LIVERPOOL JMU LIBRARY

Sport, Health and the Body in the History of Education

Historians in recent years have paid considerable attention to sport and leisure in the past, and historians of education are no exception. The chapters in this book showcase the breadth and depth of scholarship in this area, bringing new perspectives to bear on the history of physical education in several different European countries. Ranging from schoolgirl cricket in early postwar England to the varying approaches to physical education in the nineteenth-century Netherlands, the contributions to this book all emphasise the importance of physical education to wider conceptions of education for citizenship. A number of chapters tackle issues in gender history, while others focus on the effects – often unintended – of policy-makers and the conflicts that could arise from the imposition of new physical education curricula. Covering England, Scotland, France, Germany, the Netherlands and Greece, this book features the work of both established and emerging scholars, and is an important contribution to the historiography of both education and sport.

This book was originally published as a special issue of *History of Education*.

Mark Freeman is a Senior Lecturer in the Department of Humanities and Social Sciences, Institute of Education, University of London. He is the co-editor of *History of Education*, and has published widely on many areas of modern British social, educational and business history. He is currently working on a collaborative AHRC-funded project entitled 'The Redress of the Past: Historical Pageants in Britain 1905–2016'.

Sport, Health and the Body in the History of Education

Edited by
Mark Freeman

Routledge
Taylor & Francis Group

LONDON AND NEW YORK

First published 2015
by Routledge
2 Park Square, Milton Park, Abingdon, Oxon, OX14 4RN, UK

and by Routledge
711 Third Avenue, New York, NY 10017, USA

Routledge is an imprint of the Taylor & Francis Group, an informa business

© 2015 Taylor & Francis

All rights reserved. No part of this book may be reprinted or reproduced
or utilised in any form or by any electronic, mechanical, or other means,
now known or hereafter invented, including photocopying and recording,
or in any information storage or retrieval system, without permission in
writing from the publishers.

Trademark notice: Product or corporate names may be trademarks or
registered trademarks, and are used only for identification and
explanation without intent to infringe.

British Library Cataloguing in Publication Data
A catalogue record for this book is available from the British Library

ISBN 13: 978-1-138-82658-8

Typeset in Times New Roman
by RefineCatch Limited, Bungay, Suffolk

Publisher's Note
The publisher accepts responsibility for any inconsistencies that may have
arisen during the conversion of this book from journal articles to book chapters,
namely the possible inclusion of journal terminology.

Disclaimer
Every effort has been made to contact copyright holders for their permission to
reprint material in this book. The publishers would be grateful to hear from any
copyright holder who is not here acknowledged and will undertake to rectify
any errors or omissions in future editions of this book.

Contents

Citation Information

The chapters in this book were originally published in *History of Education*, volume 41, no. 6 (November 2012). When citing this material, please use the original page numbering for each article, as follows:

Chapter 7

Images of the body: the Greek physical education curriculum since the Second World War
Dimitris Foteinos
History of Education, volume 41, no. 6 (November 2012) pp. 807–822

Please direct any queries you may have about the citations to
clsuk.permissions@cengage.com

Notes on Contributors

Heather L. Dichter received her PhD in History from the University of Toronto, Canada, in 2008 and is Assistant Professor in the Department of Sport Management and Media at Ithaca College, USA. Her work explores the intersection of sport and politics in postwar Europe. She has published articles in *Stadion* and the *International Journal for the History of Sport* and co-edited, with Bruce Kidd, a special issue of *Sport in Society* on Olympic Reform. She also co-edited, with Andrew Johns, *Diplomatic Games*, an anthology on sport and foreign relations after 1945 published by the University Press of Kentucky.

Dimitris Foteinos is currently working as an Assistant Professor at the University of Athens, Greece, Faculty of Philosophy-Pedagogy-Psychology. His research interests are in the history of education in Greece, and in particular he is focusing on the history of curricula, school knowledge and the politics of knowledge.

Willeke Los is Assistant Professor in the History of Humanism at the University of Humanistic Studies, Utrecht, the Netherlands.

Eilidh H.R. Macrae recently completed her doctoral thesis in Economic and Social History at the University of Glasgow and is now a Lecturer in Sports Development at Abertay University, Dundee, Scotland.

Rafaelle Nicholson is a PhD student at Queen Mary, University of London, UK, researching the history of women's cricket in Britain since 1945. Prior to this she obtained a BA in History and Politics from Merton College, Oxford, and an MSt in Women's Studies from Mansfield College, Oxford, UK.

Jean Saint-Martin is a Professor at the University of Strasbourg, France. His research encompasses history and cultural studies and embraces the development of physical education and school sports in Europe during the nineteenth- and twentieth-centuries. It also explores both the origins and changes in body technics within leisure activities, with a particular focus on gymnastic movements and outdoor sports.

Vincent Stolk is an Historian. He is currently working as a PhD Researcher at the J.P. van Praag Institute, University of Humanistic Studies, Utrecht, the Netherlands. His research interests include the history of freethought, modern humanism and education.

Thierry Terret is Professor of Sports History and the Director of the Centre for Research and Innovation in Sport (CRIS) at the University of Lyon, France. His main research interests are sport and gender, sport and politics, and sport and European trans-culturality. His most recent publications include *Histoire du sport et géopolitique*

(Paris: L'Harmattan, 2011) and, together with J.A. Mangan, *Sport, Militarism and the Great War: Martial Manliness and Armageddon* (London: Routledge, 2012).

Wiel Veugelers is Professor of Education at the University of Humanistic Studies, Utrecht and Associate Professor of Curriculum Studies at the University of Amsterdam, the Netherlands. His research interests are education and Humanism, moral development, citizenship education, and educational change.

INTRODUCTION

Sport, health and the body in the history of education

Most of the articles in this special issue of *History of Education* were originally presented at the History of Education Society annual conference, held at Glasgow University Union in November 2011. This conference attracted delegates from more than 10 countries, and the subject matter of the papers ranged even more widely. It was the first time that the Society's conference had been held in Scotland, and the occasion was used to launch a new research network, Historians of Education in Scotland (HEdScot), funded by the Royal Society of Edinburgh.

The theme of the conference was 'Sport, Health and the Body in the History of Education'. The history of sport and leisure is a flourishing area of historical research, with a number of journals dedicated to it, including *Sport in History* and the *International Journal of the History of Sport*. The latter, remarkably, is published 18 times a year. Historians of education have participated fully in the growth of interest in sport in recent years. A burgeoning historiography of physical education (PE) in many cultures and contexts, and broadly defined, has brought new breadth to the history of education. In this journal, articles on physical education in interwar Scotland, school playgrounds in Sweden in the 1970s, outdoor education in post-war Britain and gymnastics in nineteenth-century Hungarian schools give an idea of the range of interests that have been represented under this broad heading.[1] Nevertheless, Gary McCulloch's recent survey of 40 years of articles on secondary education in this journal shows that physical education and the school curriculum has not featured significantly, although there has been a longstanding interest in 'muscular Christianity' and the athleticism of the late Victorian public school.[2]

It is appropriate, then, that a particular focus of the articles collected in this issue is on physical education, sport and gymnastics in schools in various European countries – France, Germany, Greece, Scotland, England and the Netherlands – since the nineteenth century. As John Welshman emphasised in an important article published in 1998 and dealing with England and Wales in the period 1900–1940, 'physical education and sport had an enhanced significance since they overlapped with wider concerns and issues', notably an interest in 'education for citizenship'

---

[1]Fiona Skillen, '"A Sound System of Physical Training": The Development of Girls' Physical Education in Interwar Scotland', *History of Education* 38 (2009): 403–18; Anna Larsson, 'A Children's Place? The School Playground Debate in Postwar Sweden', *History of Education* (forthcoming); Mark Freeman, 'From "Character-Training" to "Personal Growth": The Early History of Outward Bound 1941–1965', *History of Education* 40 (2011): 21–43; Miklos Hadas, 'The Rationalisation of the Body: Physical Education in Hungary in the Nineteenth Century', *History of Education* 38 (2009): 61–77.
[2]Gary McCulloch, 'The History of Secondary Education in *History of Education*', *History of Education* 41 (2012): 25–39, esp. p. 35.

that was a key feature of this period.[3] The same holds true, as the articles in this issue show, across other periods and in other geographical contexts. The culture and curriculum of PE bears the influences of wider discourses and political priorities, and has often – as the cases of Greece and France, discussed in these pages, clearly demonstrate – been seen to serve a particular national interest. Although PE is by no means unique among school subjects in this respect, the ways in which cultural and political influences have affected its development are of particular interest, offering as they do insights into other areas of historical inquiry, notably histories of health, medicine and the body.[4]

The articles by Vincent Stolk *et al.* and Thierry Terret and Jean Saint-Martin both consider the intellectual influences on PE in specific European contexts. Stolk *et al.* consider nineteenth-century Dutch freethinkers and their approach to PE, and their article shows how the main objectives of this school of thought were to promote 'humanity and individual development' rather than 'the main interests of the state'. This strand of Dutch thought, drawing heavily on the German concept of *Bildung*, focused on the promotion of 'natural education', in contrast to a parallel tradition that emphasised the social usefulness of PE and its role in the creation of good citizens. Terret and Saint-Martin examine the 'French method' and its role in supporting French cultural imperialism: the 'method' was successfully exported to Brazil, for example. The international dimension of PE cultures is an important aspect of educational history. As Welshman has noted, concerns about the faster development of PE in the continental dictatorships were a significant motivation among British policy-makers in the 1930s, when attempts were made to preserve Britain's status as one of the 'leading nations' by enhancing the PE curriculum. Importantly, though, some aspects of the German and Russian systems did not find favour, being, in the words of a British government White Paper in 1936, 'wholly alien to the national temper and tradition'.[5] This emphasises the importance of specific national cultures in the history of education: although international influences have been widely felt, the national context has been at least as important in the ways in which PE has evolved. This is emphasised in the article in this issue by Dimitris Foteinos on the history of the modern Greek PE curriculum, which has served the political and ideological aims of the modern state, through a particular set of practices that have been considered to reflect the traditions of the ancient Greek world. According to Foteinos, in both dictatorial and liberal democratic regimes in modern Greece, PE curricula have incorporated practices that aim at the cultural 'indoctrination' of young people. These have taken various forms, including traditional Greek dancing, military-style drill and education in particular Olympic sports; in the most recent period they have aimed at promoting multiculturalism and global citizenship. Foteinos argues that it is these practices that have enabled PE to find a more secure and respected place within the curriculum, although at the same time other key objectives, notably the promotion of healthy lifestyles, seem to have been undermined.

---

[3]John Welshman, 'Physical Culture and Sport in Schools in England and Wales 1900–40', *International Journal of the History of Sport* 15 (1998): 60.
[4]An earlier special issue of *History of Education* (36, no. 2, 2007) dealt with 'The Body of the Schoolchild in the History of Education'.
[5]Welshman, 'Physical Culture', 68–71.

These themes recur in Heather Dichter's article on the 'rebuilding' of PE in the Western-occupied zones of Germany in the immediate aftermath of the Second World War. Here, the occupation powers found themselves dealing with the complex legacy of Nazi education, among which was a focus on 'militarised sport' in the PE curriculum. The creation of the *Deutsche Sportshochschule* to educate PE teachers was a vital part of the denazification programme, and it became a lasting legacy of the occupation. Its aim was to embed a more democratic version of PE into West German culture, and it seems to have had considerable early success. The occupation powers, particularly the Americans and British, believed that sport had an important role to play in fostering democracy in post-war Germany, and this echoes experiences in other countries, where the cultural impact of PE has been an important part of policy-makers' thinking.

Although most of the articles in this issue focus on the motivations of those who developed the PE and sport curriculum, Eilidh H.R. Macrae's article on the education of Scottish girls, considering mainly the post-war period, uses oral evidence to assess the pupils' perspectives on the impact of educational policy. Macrae strikingly reveals the 'minimal' facilities available in terms of changing facilities, and the widespread ignorance of their own bodies that prevailed among many young women in Scotland at this time. Some of her findings echo those of an article by Angela Davis, published in *History of Education* in 2008.[6]

Using different sources, Rafaelle Nicholson shows that the perception of schoolgirls among educational officials in England was at odds with the experience of girls themselves: a demand for cricket existed among many girls and young women, which was not satisfied, 'due to the entrenched conservative attitudes of the educational authorities and some teachers'. In both England and Scotland there was a marked reluctance to invest in facilities for girls' sport, reflecting the persistence of powerfully gendered approaches to physical education.

The articles in this special issue focus on one area of 'Sport, Health and the Body in the History of Education'; much more productive work has been, and remains to be, done under this broad theme. It is to be hoped that the publication of this collection of papers from the History of Education Society's annual conference will present opportunities for further studies of PE in different cultural and political contexts, and that the history of sport and the body will remain an area of interest for historians of education.

Mark Freeman
University of Glasgow, UK

---

[6]Angela Davis, "'Oh no, Nothing, we didn't Learn Anything": Sex Education and the Preparation of Girls for Motherhood c.1930–1970', *History of Education* 37 (2008): 661–77.

Journey in the historiography of the *French Method of Physical Education*: a matter of nationalism, imperialism and gender

Thierry Terret[a] and Jean Saint-Martin[b]

[a]Centre for Research and Innovation in Sport (CRIS), University of Lyon 1, Lyon, France; [b]Faculty of Sport Sciences, University of Strasbourg, France

The three volumes of the *French Method of Physical Education* were published by the military school of Joinville-Le-Pont between 1925 and 1927 and became one of the most successful reference materials in France for sport and physical education among school, military and civilian institutions. Several authors studied these manuals, but they focused mainly on their pedagogic eclecticism and philosophical background. They also stressed that the Army accepted to reduce its military goal in order to fulfil the hygienic aims that the country considered crucial in the post-war context. Only recently, however, have new perspectives begun exploring more systematically the French Method in its social, political, gender and international aspects. The aim of this paper is to propose a first synthesis of these works and, together with some new insights, to free the French Method from the purely pedagogic history in which it has long remained within the historiography of education.

Introduction

At the end of 1918, with the war barely finished, the High Commissioner charged the Military School of Joinville with the task of renewing the former programme of physical education which dated back to 1910.[1] The aim was 'to establish a general method of physical education applicable to all French people without distinction of age or sex and adapted to the national temperament'.[2] This *Projet de règlement de la méthode française* was drawn up by several people, including servicemen at Joinville, but also civilian gymnastics instructors and doctors.[3] The first of the seven parts that made up the publication concerned children from four to 14 years old and appeared in 1919, with the subsequent parts being published over the following three years. These texts were revised several times with the final version

---

[1]This article forms part of a research programme financed by The Agence Nationale de la *Recherche* (French National Research Agency, ANR-08-VULN-001/PRAS-GEVU).
[2]Ministère de la Guerre, *Règlement général d'éducation physique. Méthode française* (Paris: Charles-Lavauzelle, 1925), Vol. 1.
[3]It is nowadays still impossible to know who exactly wrote every part of the French Method. Among the probable authors were Lieutenant-Colonel See and Colonel Bonvalot who were in charge of the Military School of Joinville respectively from 1919 to 1921 and from 1921 to 1928, and Dr Colonel Maurice Boigey for the scientific parts of volume 1.

being drafted in 1925, though their publication in 800 pages and three volumes took several years, from 1925 to 1928.

In its most successful version, the French method included three volumes. The first presented its scientific and educational foundations, together with the characteristics of the method for people under 18, whilst the second focused on 'higher' physical education and the introduction to sport for older children. The third volume, with its last section on re-education being deleted for unknown reasons, concerned military physical education and included a series of appendices on the role of doctors and instructors.

The French method was warmly acknowledged by the political authorities from the very beginning. In 1925, the first volume of the *French Method of Physical Education* was immediately approved by the Ministry of War. Two years earlier, when directives had reformed the elementary school system in France and strongly modified educational methods and curricula, they had stipulated that primary school teachers should refer to the *Projet de règlement de la méthode française* for physical education.[4] The publication of the French method also occurred at a time when France was trying to build a secondary school system with no cost to its families, to make physical education compulsory in colleges and high schools, and to extend the volume of physical education by adding a weekly half-day of outdoor activities.[5]

According to the French historiography of sport and physical education,[6] most of the historians who initially wrote on the French method of physical education were deeply influenced by the history of thought and the history of pedagogy,[7] with the exceptions of Jacques Thibault's essay on ego-history[8] and the more contextualised approach used by Marcel Spivak in his doctoral thesis on the social history of military sport.[9] Within the last 15 years, however, new perspectives have begun exploring more systematically the French method in its social, political, gender and international aspects. Often written by a generation of historians more familiar with cultural and political history, these latest insights, which also structure the current paper, provide a wider view on the significance of the French method.

---

[4]'Instructions du 20 juin 1923 relatives au nouveau plan d'études des écoles primaires élémentaires', in *Bulletin Administratif du Ministère de l'Instruction Publique* (Paris: Imprimerie nationale, 1er août 1923).

[5]Most of these measures were taken in 1925, the very same year the first volume of the French Method was published.

[6]Thierry Terret, 'Is there a French Sport Historiography?, *International Journal of the History of Sport* 28, no. 14 (2011): 2061–84.

[7]Jacques Ulmann, *De la gymnastique aux sports modernes, histoire des doctrines de l'éducation physique* (Paris: Vrin, 1965); Jacques Thibault, *Sport et éducation physique, 1870–1970. Influence du mouvement sportif sur l'évolution de l'éducation physique dans l'enseignement secondaire français* (Paris: Vrin, 1972); Gilbert Andrieu, *L'éducation physique au XXe siècle: une histoire des pratiques* (Paris: Actio, 1990); Ministère de la Défense, État-major des armées, *Une histoire culturelle du sport, De Joinville à l'Olympisme* (Paris: Ed. revue *EP.S.*, 1996); Pierre Simonet, *L'INSEP. De la gymnastique joinvillaise aux sports contemporains* (Paris: G. Klopp, 1998).

[8]Jacques Thibault, *Itinéraire d'un professeur d'éducation physique* (Clermont-Ferrand: AFRAPS, 1992).

[9]Marcel Spivak, *Education, Sport et Nationalisme en France du Second Empire au Front populaire: un aspect original de la défense nationale* [Education, Sport and Nationalism in France from the Second Empire to the Popular Front: a unique aspect of National Defence] (unpublished dissertation, University Paris 1-Sorbonne, 1983).

The aim of this paper is to present an overview of these works. It first presents how the French method has rather been described as a pedagogic consensus to end the 'war of methods'. It then shows how the studies have progressively been freed from the purely pedagogic history in which they have long remained within the historiography of education, and link the new trends of this historiographical survey to more recent inflexions of both the history of education and cultural history in general.[10] In doing so the French method appears to have been a vehicle for nationalism, imperialism and gender norms, thus reflecting some of France's key issues of the interwar period.

The French method of physical education and so-called 'war of methods'

Several authors, mainly historians of physical education, have studied the French method of physical education between the mid-1960s and the mid-1990s. Their works presented a number of similarities. They mainly focused on the pedagogic eclecticism and philosophical background of the method. They also stressed that the goal of the method was both military-oriented as it was written by a military institution and health-oriented in order to fulfil the hygienic aims that France considered crucial in the post-war context. With the percentage of under-25s reaching 11.5% of the French population[11] and the terrible statement that an average of one man in 26 had not come back from the Front,[12] alongside a worrying level of health in general, everything had to be done to save the 'French race'.[13] Finally these authors argued that the French method strove to modernise physical education by using different gymnastics traditions and concepts.

Most of these early studies on the French method insisted on its role to end the so-called war of methods which France underwent in the field of physical education in the early 1920s. From this point of view physical education as set down by the school of Joinville achieved a consensus, unthinkable prior to the war, through a method which integrated not only the traditional references of military preparation, based on the legacy of Francisco Amoros, but also references to Swedish gymnastics, brought to France by physician Philippe Tissié.[14] Added to these were references to the Natural method that Georges Hébert had succeeded in establishing in the eyes of the political authorities immediately prior to the war, together with the introduction to sport and scientific constructions of Georges Demenÿ who, when he died in 1917, left behind him an extensive knowledge base concerning rational

[10]Although the paper is mainly based on a survey of the literature it also includes primary sources more appositely when such details sound appropriate or when the discussion refers to some of the authors' own works.

[11]André Armengaud, *La population française au XXe siècle* (Paris: PUF, 1965).

[12]Serge Berstein and Pierre Milza, *Histoire de l'Europe contemporaine. De l'Europe du XIXe siècle à l'Europe d'aujourd'hui* (Paris: Hatier, 2002); François Guedj, Stéphane Sirot, eds, *Histoire sociale de l'Europe. Industrialisation et société en Europe occidentale. 1880–1970* (Paris: Seli Arslan, 1997).

[13]As an example, Colonel Marchal's *Comment on refait une race* (Paris: Tallandier, 1930) was so successful that it was edited five times during the interwar period.

[14]Simonet, L'INSEP; Jean Saint-Martin, Yves Travaillot, Pierre-Alban Lebecq and Yves Morales, *Philippe Tissié et la croisade sociale en Education physique. 1888–1914* (Bordeaux: Presses Universitaires de Bordeaux, in press 2012).

physical education, on which the authors of the French Method drew without restraint.[15]

In more precise detail, the first part of a physical education lesson was devoted exclusively to so-called 'educative gymnastics' ('gymnastique de formation') and included limbering-up exercises mixed with asymmetrical exercises that were to be done in a 'comprehensive and rounded manner', hence applying the recommendations of Georges Demenÿ, as well as following the powerful Swedish influence.[16] The second part of the lesson, also referred to as 'applied gymnastics' ('gymnastique d'application'), merged most of Hébert's Natural method with intermittent educational and preparatory exercises, and formed a sort of ill-defined transition between the Natural method and sport. Just as if, by comparison, with music theory being learnt during the first half of the lesson, the second half would teach the child to play based on a well-defined melody and music score. And so, multi-scale gymnastics gave way to applied gymnastics, where the notion of play gradually dwindled away.

Association of the terms eclecticism and French, in their capacity as the two main notions of the national method established in France in the middle of the reconstruction period, constituted a sort of 'ideal summary of Europe, a quiet force of all syntheses', as mentioned by Anne-Marie Thiesse.[17] Yet the drawing up of this pedagogic doctrine immediately reopened old conflicts. The partisans of each method commented, often in a critical manner, upon the way in which their ideas were borrowed for the purposes of this eclecticism which, according to Philippe Tissié in 1922, represented a 'babel of systems, where each one speaks a language they wish to impose and where aggressive emotionalism bars the way to constraining educational reason'.[18] Although those in charge at the School of Joinville were endeavouring to bring together the different currents existing in France in terms of physical education theory, the result obtained appeared to be quite the opposite of what had been intended. Albeit designed with the aim of putting an end to the 'war between systems'[19] which had been raging since the pre-war period, the French Method reignited rather than attenuated it.

Despite this failure, there was no doubt for Joinville that the quest for pedagogic consensus concealed a number of more political ambitions aiming to consolidate weakened legitimacy. Indeed, wishing to forget the horrors of the trenches at the end of the war, France witnessed the development of a major pacifist movement.[20] In terms of education the military institution as a whole was marginalised more than before 1914 and came up, more especially, against the stronger competition of pressure from medical and health fields, supported as it was by the context of body reconstruction in the 1920s. Over and beyond elements borrowed from the main

---

[15]Gilles Bui-Xuân, Jacques Gleyse, *De l'émergence de l'éducation physique, G. Demenÿ et G. Hébert* (Paris: Hatier, 2001); Jean-Michel Delaplace, *Georges Hébert, sculpteur de corps* (Paris: Vuibert, 2005).

[16]Jean Saint-Martin, 'La perception de la méthode suédoise et ses conséquences sur le développement de la gymnastique française (1815–1914)', *Stadion* XXVII (2001): 169–78.

[17]Anne-Marie Thiesse, 'La fabrication culturelle des nations européennes', in *L'identité*, ed. Bruno Choc (Paris: Sciences Humaines éditions, 2004), 283.

[18]Philippe Tissié, *L'éducation physique rationnelle* (Paris, Alcan, 1922), 39.

[19]Elie Mercier, 'De l'hérédité en éducation physique', in *Encyclopédie des sports*, ed. Académie des sports (Paris: Librairie de France, vol. 1, 1924), 234.

[20]Antoine Prost, *Les anciens combattants. 1914–1940* (Paris: Gallimard, 1977).

currents of the time, the authors of the French Method sought consensus by establishing health as the primary aim of physical education. For the youngest in particular the method sought, first and foremost, to develop the principal functions of breathing, circulation and joint movement without building excessively big muscles. Health concerns of the Joinville physical education programme benefited, however, from the rise of a Eugenics movement which justified the urgency for educational action and explained the emergence of a position which associated the French Method and health with recovery of the *race*.[21]

Thus, when Henri de Bellefon and Gabriel Marul claimed that the French Method 'is perfectly appropriate for the character of our race',[22] their declaration fully echoed calls from all sides for the regeneration of a decimated population. In order to cope with the 1.4 million lives lost during the war, each and every one called on the energy of all, whether it be for the rebuilding of 'specifically purebred humans as handsome as horse thoroughbreds'[23] for military networks or in the case of requests from Frantz Reichel, figurehead of French sport during the immediate postwar period, calling for 'young people to have one hour of physical exercise per day, two afternoons of sport per week and sports fields',[24] rather than building new hospitals.

Several voices made themselves heard in Parliament. Henri Paté, who was appointed as Commissioner for Physical Education, Sport and Military Preparation on 16 January 1921 and, as such, was part of the Ministry of War,[25] wished to force French young people to develop their body, force and courage.[26] As founder of a short-lived national committee on physical education and social hygiene, he denounced, on several occasions, the 'embryonic stage' of the principle of compulsory physical education in schools while,[27] at the same time, promoting the Preliminary Drafts of General Rules for Physical Education, which would become the French Physical Education Method in 1925.[28] The deputy Adolphe Chéron, also an

---

[21]Jacques Defrance, 'L'eugénisme et la culture scientifique dans le champ des activités physiques et des sports (1910–1950)', in *Entre le social et le vital. L'éducation physique et sportive sous tensions. XVIIIe–XXe siècle)*, ed. Christian Pociello (Grenoble: Presses universitaires de Grenoble, 2004), 127–60.

[22]Henri de Bellefon and Gabriel Marul, *La méthode française d'éducation physique, Manuel pratique* (Paris: E. Chiron, 1935), 2 (Prologue). These two were military instructors in Joinville at the time the French Method was written and they probably contributed to it.

[23]*Le Soldat de demain*, February 1, 1920, 37.

[24]Frantz Reichel, 'Pour la Race', *Le Figaro* (January 13, 1919).

[25]Jacques Defrance, 'Henry Paté et l'engagement de l'Etat dans le champ de l'éducation physique et des sports (1918–1930)', *Cahiers d'histoire* 2 (2002): 54–78. According to Jacques Defrance, Henry Paté was 'very right oriented, he (was) anti-German and anti-Mussolini'. Close to Louis Barthou, fighting against both socialists and right-wing nationalists, he was part of the radical republican movement. In the 1930s, he fell under the influence of the new right wing, which had broken away from the patriotic nationalist themes of the years 1890–1920, drawing inspiration from American modernism, and became close to André Tardieu. For French sport sociologist Jacques Defrance, his political opportunism moved him further and further to the right.

[26]*Journal Officiel. Débats Parlementaires. Chambre* [JODPC], 23 May 1919, Annexe n° 6184, 1625.

[27]See for instance *L'Ere nouvelle* (July 20, 1920).

[28]JODPC, 23 May 1919, Annexe n° 6184, 1625–1626.

ardent supporter of physical education as preparation for the army,[29] in turn called for a method that would allow the building of 'strong, dexterous and resilient men, endowed with tenacious energy'.[30] The same positions were defended by the Union des Grandes Associations Françaises pour l'Essor National (Union of Major French Associations for National Development), with one of its members being Colonel Bonvalot who was, moreover, Major of the Joinville School:

> Through physical education, we are seeking to prepare those young people who will, when the time comes, become soldiers.... Practising sport gives understanding and first-hand experience of the necessity for discipline, it results in people practising it willingly and accustoms them, subsequently, to comply with social rules observed more closely by the French, since they will not be imposed by force, but rather agreed to through reason and good will.[31]

Yet, from defence of the race to the nationalist cause was only one step, which promoters of the French Method promptly took.

French method, France and nationalism

In the early 1990s new investigations were made in the archives of the Ministry of Foreign Affairs, which showed the connection between physical education, nationalism and political power. Although the approach remained largely influenced by social history the understanding of the French method was impacted by this new corpus of empirical data. Jean Saint-Martin, a former physical education teacher whose PhD was supervised by pioneer of French sports history Pierre Arnaud, explored in particular the alliances between military and educational institutions and the social positions of their leaders.[32] He found out that many influential people in the field of sport and physical education of the early 1920s, such as Philippe Tissié, Charles Cazalet and Adolphe Chéron, were members of the Union des grandes associations françaises pour l'essor national,[33] headed by the President of the Republic himself, Raymond Poincaré. Its treasurer, Léon Robelin, was moreover secretary general of the very powerful Teaching League (Ligue de l'Education).[34] Its institutional members included the societies for physical culture, shooting and sport, whose vice-president was the radical socialist Roger Trousselle, one of the undisputed figureheads of French colonial ideology.[35]

---

[29]Adolphe Chéron was the president of the Union des Sociétés d'Education Physique et de Préparation au Service Militaire, founded in 1885 and whose journal *Le Soldat de demain* often exalted the importance of physical education as a preparation for war.

[30]*JODPC*, 2nd Extraordinary session, December 10, 1920, Annexe n° 1792, 568.

[31]Archives of the French Foreign Office [Ministère des Affaires Etrangères – MAE], SOFE File 90: *L'Ecole et l'Armée* (Paris: Bulletin officiel bimestriel de la Fédération des sociétés de culture physique, de tir et de sports, June 1923), 104.

[32]Jean Saint-Martin, *L'éducation physique à l'épreuve de la Nation (1918–1939)* (Paris: Vuibert, 2005).

[33]This organisation was founded in 1875 and aimed at the promotion and dissemination of French *savoir faire*.

[34]Archives MAE, SOFE, File 90.

[35]Claude Ageron, Jacques Thobie, Gilbert Meynier, Catherine Coquery-Vidrovitch, *Histoire de la France coloniale* (Paris: A. Colin, 1990); Raoul Girardet, *L'idée coloniale en France de 1871 à 1962* (Paris: Hachette, 1990).

In such a context, a widespread pro-military movement, which was very present within the School of Joinville, envisaged explicit development between the various practices in physical education and military preparation for the young, with the aim of saving the nation and engendering a renascence of the country.[36] Adolphe Chéron relentlessly defended such ideas, both at the National Assembly and within the French Olympic Committee. On 18 May 1926, for example, he protested once more against the split between physical education and military preparation:

> Sports training and physical education have social and rational consequences that the country comprehends and as a result of which it has been possible to establish authority vis-à-vis the political authorities: it is military preparation which has the effect of training young people for the purposes of national defence.[37]

His words were echoed by Gaston Vidal, Under Secretary of State for Technical Education, responsible for sport and education, and last president of the main sports federation of the country, the *Union des Sociétés Françaises de Sports Athlétiques* (USFSA) (French Federation for Athletic Sports), when he more simply considered that the French Method would shorten military service.[38]

In response to allegations in the foreign press that France had been left battered by the war, Gaston Vidal went on to claim that the French Method would contribute to the national cause by placing the country in top position on the international scene.[39] The French Method thus conveyed, in the field of corporeality, the 'defensive patriotism'[40] of physical education programmes, while ensuring greater integration of its teaching in schools. Henri de Bellefon and Gabriel Marul underlined, more particularly, the geosymbolic challenges of the method by confirming the predominant role of foreign nations in its development:

> It is because they were trained in sport that the British and the Americans were able to become good soldiers quickly.... If our children are trained, despite there not being many of them, we can, without fear, envisage a reduction of our military expenditure; no one will dare to do anything against us. Granted, we have often cried out 'war against war', but physical education will be the one that kills war.[41]

According to Saint-Martin, such national interest could, however, most likely be further explained in view of the beginning of a period of 'Franco-German cold war'[42] (1920–1923). Against a background of opposition over the issue of war debt repayment, intense anti-French propaganda developed across the Rhine, clearly well

---

[36]Albert Surier, *Forts par la culture physique, méthode française pratique et individuelle avec planches d'exercices* (Paris: Bibliothèque du colisée, 1920), prologue by A. Chéron. Albert Surier was a regular author in the anti-German journal *Le Soldat de Demain*.

[37]Archives of the French Olympic Committee [Comité National Olympique et Sportif Français – CNOSF], Minutes, May 18, 1926, Volume 9, 47.

[38]Archives of the CNOSF, Minutes, May 18, 1926, Volume 9, 48.

[39]*L'Ere nouvelle* (August 30, 1920).

[40]Olivier Loubes, *L'école et la patrie* (Paris: Belin, 2001).

[41]Bellefon and Marul, *La méthode française d'éducation physique*, 346–7.

[42]Raymond Poidevin and Jacques Bariéty, *Les relations franco-allemandes 1815–1975* (Paris: A. Colin, 1977), 240–57.

attested to by the detailed observations of the French consul in Berlin.[43] German propaganda engaged, for instance, in formal attacks on French school textbooks.[44] Hence the reaction when physical education in Germany shifted towards becoming pre-military, thus bypassing Article 177 of the Treaty of Versailles.[45] From the early 1920s onwards, in order to maintain peace in Europe at all costs and avoid 'Jahn starting his old tricks again',[46] those in charge of French physical education criticised all German initiatives,[47] to the point of alarming the sports press such as the *Miroir des sports* which described German sport as 'an ersatz of military service' in its issue published on 16 June 1921. By being published in 1925, the very same year that Germany was celebrating the millennium of the Rhineland and the annexing of the Rhineland to Germany, the French Method in fact constituted a symbolic response to what the French considered to be acts of aggression from yesterday's enemy. Its publication was even considered a success justifying the optimism of the political class. According to Henri Paté:

> The task begun during the stormy period is now finished; the general rules for physical education, approved by the Ministers of War and Public Instruction, have been published; the section on method, which has so long been researched, is finally ready and is called the French Physical Education Method.[48]

However, as international comparisons have shown, the choice of naming the method 'French' had obviously more to do with nationalism than with pedagogy.[49]

French method and the need for sport success

At the beginning of the interwar period, sport in France underwent a period of intense restructuring, which confirmed a general shift towards specialisation at the same time as its access to mass culture.[50] In addition, it found itself, more particu-

---

[43]Archives MAE, Ambassy of Berlin, File 467: 'Propagande contre la France (1921–1928)'. The many brochures collected in Germany and dispatched to Paris by the diplomatic services expressed violent criticism against the *Diktat* of Versailles and French will to regain France's geopolitical hegemony. Propaganda against the Foreign Legion was particularly intense, in order to dissuade Germans from joining it. French troops were represented by photos and caricatures of Negro soldiers, thus combining negrophobia and German nationalism. See Jean Saint-Martin, *Sports, éducations physiques et identité française. 1866–1945* (Lyon: Habilitation, University of Lyon, 2006).

[44]Archives MAE, SOFE, File 105.

[45]Jean Saint-Martin, 'La perception française de l'éducation physique allemande entre 1918 et 1935: réalité ou utopie?', in *Le sport français dans l'Entre-deux-guerres*, ed. Jean Saint-Martin and Thierry Terret (Paris: L'Harmattan, 2000), 163–93.

[46]*Le Soldat de Demain*, April 1919, 178. The author referred to the use of military gymnastics known as *Turnen* in early nineteenth-century Germany.

[47]Jean Saint-Martin, 'La perception française de l'éducation physique allemande'.

[48]Bellefon and Marul, *La méthode française d'éducation physique*. III.

[49]The strong similarities between the French and Italian systems of physical education were for instance studied by Thierry Terret and Roberta Vescovi, 'L'éducation physique à l'école primaire pendant l'entre-deux-guerres. Une comparaison des systèmes français et italiens', in *The History of Educational Institutions, Physical Education and Sport*, ed E. Trangbaeck and A. Krüger (Copenhagen: CESH, 1999), 269–83.

[50]Philippe Tétart, *Histoire du sport en France, Du Second Empire au régime de Vichy* (Paris: Vuibert, 2007).

larly, propelled to the rank of tool for national prestige, of diplomatic lever and reflection of the state of international relations, as was argued by French Pierre Arnaud and English James Riordan in a programmatic work published in 1998.[51] Not that sport had never been used in this way on certain occasions previously, but rising nationalism after 1918, in not only democracies but also totalitarian states, unquestionably gave a whole new tone to sports events and turned stadiums into a place for revenge. Several monographs on the Inter-Allied Games of 1919, the Olympic Games of Antwerp in 1920 and those of Paris four years later confirmed it: the pacifist ideology of sport conveyed by Coubertin could do little against recent memories of the trenches.[52] Moreover, Germany was not invited to the Olympic festival until the country's reinstatement by the International Olympic Committee in 1925 and its entry into the Society of Nations.

As early as January 1920, France set up a Service des œuvres françaises à l'étranger (SOFE) (service responsible for French works abroad) within the Tourism and Sport Department of the Ministry of Foreign Affairs, with the aim of restoring and strengthening the country's image through sports propaganda, while informing the government of any initiatives taken in terms of sport beyond national borders. The second volume of the French Method, dedicated to sport education, thus put into practice statements made by Gaston Vidal on 29 July 1920 that 'sport has become a state matter'[53] or those made at a slightly earlier time by Georges Noblemaire, deputy of the Hautes-Alpes region, for whom:

> It is also absolutely essential that France should not lose in the eyes of the athletic world, predominant in many countries such as America, England and Scandinavian countries, the prestige it has been given by the supreme sport of war.[54]

In this context, preparation of the nation's sports elites, which had been mainly left to private initiatives prior to the war, took on new importance. It just so happened that this task was given to the army, and more particularly the Military School of Joinville. This was particularly surprising in France, given that the military institution had long been averse to using sport in the preparation of its troops.[55] Yet, for French military officers in charge, the fact that sport was used on a large scale by British and American forces and was encouraged by the High Command acted as a trigger.[56] In

---

[51]Pierre Arnaud and James Riordan, eds, *Sport et relations internationales. 1900–1941* (Paris: L'Harmattan, 1998), 15.

[52]Thierry Terret, *Les Jeux interalliés de 1919. Sport, guerre et relations internationales* (Paris: L'Harmattan, 2002); Roland Renson, *La VIIième olympiade. Anvers 1920. Les Jeux ressuscités* (Bruxelles: Comité Olympique et Interfédéral Belge, 1995); Thierry Terret, ed., *Les Paris des Jeux olympiques de 1924* (Biarritz: Atlantica, 2008).

[53]*Le Miroir des sports* (July 29, 1920), 50.

[54]JODPC, 'Document parlementaires, annexe n° 802', Minutes April 20, 1920, 855.

[55]Spivak, *Education, Sport et nationalisme en France*.

[56]Arnaud Waquet, 'Le football des Poilus: analyse de la diffusion du football dans l'armée française au cours de la Grande Guerre', *Stadion* XXXVI (2010); Arnaud Waquet and Thierry Terret, 'Ballons ronds, Tommies et tranchées: l'impact de la présence britannique dans la diffusion du football association au sein des villes de garnison de la Somme et du Pas-de-Calais (1915–1918)', *Modern and Contemporary France* XIV, no. 4 (2006): 449–64. Thierry Terret, 'Le rôle des Young Men's Christian Associations (YMCA) dans la diffusion du sport en France pendant la Première Guerre mondiale', in *Sports, éducation physique et mouvements affinitaires*, ed. Pierre-Alban Lebecq (Paris: L'Harmattan, vol. 1: Les pratiques affinitaires, 2004), 27–56.

discovering the potential of sport for the physical and moral education of combatants, new perspectives began to take shape, in particular for the School of Joinville, expert as it was in matters of physical education. As pointed out by Thierry Terret,[57] only a few weeks after the Armistice and exactly at the time when the draft rules for the French Method were being drawn up, the School itself was chosen as the place in Paris where the French would train and prepare for the Inter-Allied Games of June–July 1919. Following the highly satisfactory results that placed France second after the United States, the School became the country's national training centre, in view of the Olympic Games to be held in Antwerp in 1920, then in Paris in 1924.

Its expertise in education and sports training was based on two competences, including that of American trainers who had been invited to stay on in Paris after the Inter-Allied Games so that the French could benefit from their know-how and technical knowledge. Such, for example, was the case for Louis Schroeder who arrived in the country in 1919 and was immediately taken on by the School of Joinville. This superintendent of leisure activities in the town of Pittsburgh, Pennsylvania had been trained at the famous YMCA College in Springfield and was thus given the responsibility of training the French athletics team for the Olympic Games in Antwerp. The parts that Maurice Boigey had borrowed from experts across the Atlantic to write his own works on training were so great in number and so visible that Louis Schroeder reported to one of the managers in charge of the YMCA that 'Our methods of training athletes and of teaching the technique of running, jumping, throwing, swimming and boxing were copied and employed by the French trainers and coaches'.[58]

Yet, Joinville was also behind a number of more original proposals, with Maurice Boigey setting up a laboratory there to study the physiology of training.[59] He carried out many experiments on sports people, both civilian and military, and circulated his results in the form of books and articles. His *Manuel scientifique d'éducation physique* (scientific manual of physical education) was an imposing book of 616 pages published in 1923, which went on to win a prize from the Academy of Medicine. Large parts of the book were used in the text of the French Method, thus confirming the direct influence of Maurice Boigey in writing it.

The contributions of Joinville in terms of training, however, were rather limited. Although the second volume of the French Method brought the military school to the fore and justified its status as preparation centre for French teams with a view to major competitions, the various sports federations were quick to criticise the inadequacy of proposals and incompetence of the Joinville trainers. Following the Paris Olympic Games, for example, where the results of French swimmers were particularly disappointing, the leaders of the French Federation of Swimming confessed that 'The military doctors of Joinville are perhaps very good in theory and therapeutics, but ... their diagnoses certainly do not argue in favour

---

[57]Thierry Terret, *Les Jeux interalliés de 1919*.
[58]Archives YMCA (Minneapolis) AS.43: *Report of the Department of Physical Education. Société des Foyers de L'Union Franco-Américaine*, September 1, 1921– September 1, 1922.
[59]Francis Charpier, *Aux origines de la médecine du sport* [On the Origins of Sport Medicine] (unpublished dissertation, University of Lyon, 2004).

of their knowledge of the sports issues we are interested in'.[60] Without going so far as to quote his name, the accusations were aimed, in particular, at Maurice Boigey, who was perfectly capable of describing complex biological processes and churning out hygienic-dietary recommendations for sportsmen, but at a loss to propose specific training modalities in the various sports.[61] Comparison with methods developed at the same time in the United States confirmed that the French Method still promoted technically centred training, whereas the Americans adopted a more physiological and quantitative approach in the preparation of their sportsmen.[62] By offering the best national synthesis of introduction to sport and training, however, the French Method reflected both the state's new geopolitical way of looking at sport and the fragility of the cultural transfers it continued to benefit from in the 1920s.

French Method and France's imperialism

During the race for world supremacy, France built up a colonial empire, which reached its zenith just before the beginning of the First World War. As the second largest Empire just behind England, with 12 million km² of territory, France enjoyed a worldwide presence. Along with her first colonial territory, before the Napoleonic era, in North America and the West Indies, the country also benefited from a number of trading posts in India. France later launched an attempt to control large parts of Africa, Asia and Oceania.[63] At the beginning of the 1920s, the French Empire was particularly powerful in Africa, with its Occidental French Africa and Equatorial French Africa territories, Tunisia, Morocco and Algeria, as well as Madagascar, Reunion, Mayotte Island and Comoros in the Indian Ocean. To this list may be added the Asian continent, Indochina and France's Indian trading posts, together with New Caledonia and Polynesia in the Pacific, several islands and territories in the West Indies (Martinique, Guadeloupe, Saint Martin, Saint Bartholomew, Guyana), as well as other areas such as Saint Pierre and Miquelon, Djibouti, not forgetting Lebanon and places in the Middle East which were held under French mandate.

The social, economic and political division of the colonised and the colonisers was visible in all areas, and sport was no exception, as shown more and more by colonial history. During the last 15 years a series of monographs have highlighted

---

[60]*Natation* 115 (June 20, 1924).

[61]On the differences between Maurice Boigey's scientific knowledge and the trainers' empirical knowledge, see Anne Roger, *L'entraînement en athlétisme en France (1919–1973): une histoire de théoriciens?* [The Training in Athletics in France. 1919–1973] (unpublished dissertation, University of Lyon, 2003).

[62]For several examples in athletics and swimming, see Anne Roger, *L'entraînement en athlétisme en France*; Thierry Terret, 'S'entraîner en natation sportive: une histoire culturelle', in *Usages corporels et pratiques sportives aquatiques du XVIIIème siècle au XXème siècle*, ed. Laurence Munoz (Paris: L'Harmattan, vol. 2, 2008), 5–38.

[63]Jean Meyer, Jean Tarrade, Annie Rey-Goldzeiguer and Jacques Thobie, *Histoire de la France coloniale, des origines à 1914* (Paris: Armand Colin, 1990).

several points of convergence between the West Indies, Africa, the Indian Ocean and other territories.[64] They show that local populations progressively took up sport in the 1920s, but that for the mother country the French colonies were not seen as a 'reservoir' of sportsmen before the 1930s, since colonial authorities feared that sports clubs might provide a cover for political or religious activities.[65] Physical education, however, was not sport. Its potential to discipline the body and therefore the mind was recognised by the French political authorities. Therefore exporting the concept was considered when the French Method became the object of stronger proselytism throughout the French Empire. On 2 September 1924, a ministerial circular relative to physical instruction and military training made it applicable in all colonial territories. In 1930, a specific guide for physical education in the colonies was published by the School of Joinville[66] and was followed by the dissemination of the French Method in French Western Africa and in the West Indian colonies of Martinique and Guadeloupe.[67] Frenchness and gender order could then be disseminated throughout the Empire, yet with some limitations as it was strongly recommended that races be separated during the courses.

The question of influencing other nations outside the colonies had to be considered in a different light on account of the competitive and dominant cultural

---

[64]For the West Indies, see Jacques Dumont, *Sport et assimilation à la Guadeloupe (1914–1965)* (Paris: L'Harmattan, 2002); Jacques Dumont, *Sport et mouvements de jeunesse à la Martinique* (Paris: L'Harmattan, 2006). For North Africa, see Youcef Fates, *Sport et politique en Algérie* (Paris: L'Harmattan, 2009). For the West and East Africa, see Bernadette Deville-Danthu, *Le sport en noir et blanc. Du sport colonial au sport africain* (Paris: L'Harmattan, 1996); David-Claude Kemo, *Représentations, politiques et pratiques corporelles au Cameroun (1920–1996). Enjeux et paradoxes du sport et de l'éducation physique en Afrique noire* [Stakes and Paradoxes of Sport and Physical Education in Black Africa] (Unpublished PhD dissertation, University of Strasbourg, 1999); Nicolas Bancel, *Entre acculturation et révolution. Mouvements de jeunesse et sports dans l'évolution politique et institutionnelle de l'AOF. 1945–1962* [Between Acculturation and Revolution. Youth Movements and Sports in the Political and Institutional Evolution of the AOF] (Unpublished dissertation, University Paris I, 1999). For the islands of the Indian Ocean, see André-Jean Benoit, *Sport colonial* (Paris: L'Harmattan, 1996); Evelyne Combeau-Mari, *Sport et décolonisation à la réunion de 1946 à la fin des années 60* (Paris: L'Harmattan, 1998); Claude Calvini, *Histoire du sport à l'île Maurice* (Paris: L'Harmattan, 2008); Evelyne Combeau-Mari, 'Colonial Sport in Madagascar. 1896–1960', special issue of *International Journal of the History of Sport* 28, no. 12 (2011). For the other territories, see for instance Yves Leloup, *Histoire des courses de pirogues polynésiennes. De l'acculturation sportive occidentale à la ré-appropriation identitaire ma'ohi. XIXe–XXe siècle* [History of Polynesian Pirogues Races. From Western Sport Acculturation to Ma'ohi Identity] (Unpublished PhD dissertation, University of French Polynesia, 2007); Agathe Larcher-Goscha, 'Sports, colonialisme et identités nationales: premières approches du «corps à corps colonial» en Indochine (1918–1945)', in *De l'Indochine à l'Algérie. La jeunesse en mouvements des deux côtés du miroir colonial. 1940–1962*, ed. Nicolas Bancel, Daniel Denis and Youcef Fates (Paris: La Découverte, 2003), 15–31.

[65]Evelyne Combeau-Mari, 'Sport in the French Colonies (1880–1962)', *Journal of Sport History* 33, no. 1 (2006), 27–58, 34.

[66]Sous-secrétariat de l'Education physique, *L'Education physique aux colonies* (Joinville-le-Pont, Imprimerie de l'École, 1930).

[67]Deville-Danthu, *Le sport en noir et blanc*, 34; Jacques Dumont, 'Joinville aux Antilles, d'une guerre à l'autre', in *L'empreinte de Joinville*, ed. Simonet, Veray, 71.

imperialism of Great Britain, the United States and, to a certain extent, Germany.[68] The geopolitical and colonial situation resulted in an implicit sharing of the regions, thus maintaining a certain balance on a continental scale. In the case of the South American continent for example, Franco-German economic and cultural rivalry urged Germany to invest in Chile and Venezuela before the First World War, whereas France was more concerned with Colombia and Brazil where her influence in various domains was already significant and had even extended beyond the social elites of the country since its independence.[69] As a state institution, the Military School of Joinville contributed to diffusing the image and values of France world-wide sending, for instance, its experts to other countries and welcoming foreign delegations for intensive physical education courses.[70] Some countries, like Luxemburg and Portugal, even made the French method a compulsory part of their curricula.[71]

Thus the French method should be considered part of the framework that constituted the new French cultural imperialism in a time of international concurrence, as demonstrated by French Thierry Terret and Brazilian Leomar Tesche in a recent case study on Brazil.[72] There, the authors recall that before and after the First World War, Brazil was the second most favoured destination of French immigrants to Latin America, after Argentina. The presence of a French community contributed to a certain 'reserve of favourable feelings to France'.[73] Yet, it was just another element to add to the wider cultural policy developed by France towards Brazil from the 1920s onwards through the 'Alliances françaises', the network of French universities and high schools in Latin America, the French-Brazilian Institute and the French-Brazilian secondary school.[74]

At the beginning of the twentieth century, Brazil was in search of its national identity in all domains. The quest included physical education, which became a means of building 'Brazilness'. As pointed out by Brazilian historians Leomar Tesche and Artur Rambo the choice was first made by the government to look

---

[68]Gerald Gems, *The Athletic Crusade: Sport and American Cultural Imperialism* (Lincoln: Nebraska University Press, 2006); James A. Mangan, *The Games Ethic and Imperialism. Aspects of the Diffusion of an Ideal* (London: Frank Cass, 1986); Allen Guttmann, *Games and Empire: Modern Sports and Cultural Imperialism* (New York: Columbia Univ. Press, 1994); Gertrud Pfister, 'Colonialism and the Enactment of German Identity – *Turnen* in South West Africa', *Journal of Sport History* 33, no. 1 (2006): 59–83.

[69]François-Xavier Guerra, 'La lumière et ses reflets: Paris et la politique latino-américaine', in *Le Paris des étrangers depuis un siècle*, ed. André Kaspi, Antoine Marès (Paris: Imprimerie Nationale, 1989): 171–82.

[70]Jean Saint-Martin, 'L'Ecole de Joinville: Une pièce maîtresse dans le rayonnement géopolitique de l'EP française entre les deux guerres mondiales?', in *L'empreinte de Joinville*, ed. Simonet and Veray, 47–64.

[71]Commandant Labrosse, *Notice sur l'École Supérieure de Joinville-le-Pont* (Joinville: Imprimerie de l'École, 1930), 39.

[72]Thierry Terret and Leomar Tesche, 'French Gymnastics in Brazil: Dissemination, Diffusion and Relocalisation', *International Journal of the History of Sport* 26, no. 13 (2009): 1983–98.

[73]An expression frequently used by the department of Foreign Policy in France, as remarked on by Cécilia Torres, 'Les enjeux diplomatiques de l'enseignement de la langue française au Brésil', *Bulletin de l'Institut Pierre Renouvin* (1948–1961) (Winter 2003).

[74]Hugo R. Suppo, 'La politique culturelle française au Brésil entre les années 1920–1950' [The French Cultural Policy in Brazil during the years 1920–1950] (unpublished dissertation, University Paris III, 1999).

towards Europe, and more especially Germany, because the South of Brazil was more sympathetic to her.[75] However, before the First World War many teaching establishments already began to give up German *Turnen* (gymnastics) and to consider France the model to follow, especially after the hiring of a French military mission to take command of the military instruction of the Public Force of the state of São Paulo (Military Police) in 1907. The impact of the officers' presence on gymnastics in Brazil went on with the arrival of the French Military Mission to support the Brazilian Army in 1919. Two years later, a new era began for Brazil as a Republic, with many changes in both social and economic spheres of the nation.[76] At the military level, the Regulamento de Instrução Física Militar (Military Physical Instruction Regulation) was approved by a presidential decree (no. 14.784) in 1921 and paved the way for the importation of the French method.[77] The method was put into effect one year later and became more successful some years later. Indeed, in 1928, Joinville sent Major Pierre Segur to deliver a training course on the French Method.[78] This officer was influential enough to ensure the expansion of the French Method. As a consequence, General Nestor Pessoas presented a bill establishing, in 1929, that 'Physical Education shall be exercised by all residing in Brazil. It is compulsory in all federal, municipal and private teaching establishments from six years of age on for both sexes.' The text also mentioned that:

> As long as the 'National Method of Physical Education' has not been created, the so-called French method is adopted for all the Brazilian territory, under the title of 'Regulamento Geral de Educação Física' (General Regulation of Physical Education).[79]

Although Cantarino Filho made it clear that the French method did not enjoy unanimous agreement,[80] Joinville succeeded, at least for some years, in its project of disseminating its cultural values and pedagogic proposals.[81] In doing so, it contributed to enhancing France's prestige and cultural imperialism outside Europe. However, the strategic exportation of gymnastics systems was not reserved to France, when considering for instance Denmark's policy on Niels Bukh's gymnastics.[82] It was more generally already known before 1914 by countries on both sides of the

---

[75]Leomar Tesche and Artur B. Rambo, 'Reconstructing the Fatherland: German Turnen in Southern Brazil', *European Sports History Review* 3 (2001): 5–22.

[76]Bradford Burns, *A History of Brazil* (New York and London: Columbia University Press, 1993).

[77]Mario Ribeiro Cantarino Filho, 'A Educação Física no Brasil', in *Geschichte der Leibesübungen*, ed. Horst Ueberhorst (Berlin: Verlag Bartels & Wernitz GmbH, 1989), 889–911.

[78]Cantarino Filho, 'A Educação Física no Brasil', 901.

[79]Silvana.V. Goellner, 'O Método Francês e Militarização da Educação Física na Escola Brasiliera', in *Pesquisa Histórica na Educação Física Brasileira*, ed. Neto Amarílio Ferreira (Vitória: CEFD-UFES, 1996), 123–43.

[80]Cantarino Filho, *A Educação Física no Brasil*, 901.

[81]The influence of the French method of physical education finally ceased in Brazil as a result of the so-called Capanema Reform of 1946.

[82]The Danish Ambassy in Rio de Janeiro organised for instance a tour of experts in Niels Bukh's Danish system in Brazil, Argentina and Uruguay in 1938. See Hand Bonde, *Gymnastics and Politics: Niels Bukh and Male Aesthetics* (Copenhagen: Museum Tusculanum, 2006), 223.

Atlantic in their quest for power.[83] For France, it was nevertheless the first time that an official method of physical education contributed so obviously to the exportation of national norms and ideology.

French Method, hegemonic masculinity and femininity

Surfing on the fertilisation of sports history by gender studies, which has occurred since the early 2000s in France,[84] the history of the French method of physical education has more recently been the object of analyses aiming at exploring its role in the making of masculinity and femininity.[85] The results of these investigations link the gender perspectives with the war and post-war context.

In contrast with Goldstein's claim that war is a central component of masculinity and a test of manhood,[86] the Great War rather corresponded to a challenge to hegemonic masculinity.[87] For soldiers the feeling of isolation, for instance, not only created male solidarity, but also upset existing certitudes about men, women, sexuality and gender relations. The absence of wives and fiancées gave rise to a permanent feeling of frustration and even hostility towards those women who were sometimes seen to be taking advantage of the war situation.[88] Therefore, at the end of the war, the traditional relationships between men and women remained strongly influenced and destabilised by the memories of the trenches.[89] The fear of death led to a more cynical view on the world and encouraged a *carpe diem* mentality. The need to live intensely for the moment led to new types of behaviour dedicated to the 'Roaring Twenties'. Yet even as the desire for modernity became more widespread, French society tightened its grip on its traditional values by, for example, applying an ambitious pro-birth policy during the 1920s and enforcing the laws against abortion more strictly. This paradoxical situation had consequences on women's place in society: 'More than ever, feminine sexuality was locked into the mother–prostitute alternative, and the family considered as the basic unit.'[90]

Of course, the wife–mother model was not the only standard, since new role models such as Suzanne Lenglen and Marie Curie were emerging to open the way for a broader emancipation of women. Mary Louise Roberts considers that France produced three female models during the 1920s: the modern woman, source of anxiety for the patriarchal tradition; the mother, reassuring; and the chaste, unmarried

---

[83]A recent collection of essays has been entirely devoted to this question. See Gertrud Pfister, ed., *Gymnastics: a Transatlantic Movement: From Europe to America* (London: Routledge, 2010).

[84]Thierry Terret, 'Le genre dans l'histoire du sport', *Clio. Femmes, histoire, société* 23 (2006): 211–40.

[85]Thierry Terret, 'Gendering Physical Education: The Role of the French State in the Aftermath of WWI', *European Journal of Sport Science* 11, no. 5 (2011): 1–6.

[86]Joshua S. Goldstein, *War and Gender: How Gender Shapes the War System and Vice Versa* (Cambridge: Cambridge University Press, 2001).

[87]Luc Capdevila, François Rouquet, Fabrice Virgili and Danièle Voldman, *Hommes et femmes dans la France en guerre. 1914–1945* (Paris: Payot, 2003).

[88]Jean-Yves Le Naour, *Misères et tourments de la chair durant la Grande Guerre. Les mœurs sexuelles des Français, 1914–1918* (Paris: Aubier, 2002).

[89]André Rauch, *L'identité masculine à l'ombre des femmes. De la Grande Guerre à la Gay Pride* (Paris: Hachette, 2004).

[90]Françoise Thébaud, 'La Grande Guerre. Le triomphe de la division sexuelle', in *Histoire des femmes en Occident*, ed. Françoise Thébaud (Paris: Plon, 1992), vol. 5, 81–144, 116.

active woman who turned out to be the link between the past and the new society taking shape.[91] Nevertheless, the revolution was restrained and women were generally sent back to their traditional roles. It should also be kept in mind that Victor Marguerite's book *La Garçonne* ('The Flapper') may have been a great success in 1922 with a million copies sold, but its publication triggered a scandal and the author was thrown out of the French Legion of Honour.[92]

As both a military and a state institution Joinville had a unique opportunity to recall, through the French Method of Physical Education, how a man and a woman should be educated, how they should act and what was more appropriate for each of them. Yet most of the discourses of the French Method did not explicitly refer to one sex or the other. Rather they opposed the 'young' and the 'old' on the basis of physiological and biological differences organised on a six-step scale of ages. Conceptualisations of femininity and masculinity, however, were not totally absent from the text. By small touches they defined and made natural a couple of ideals where boys and girls consistently appeared in opposition to each other. In contrast to a large part of the sport press and images (postcards, posters) the pedagogic discourse of the French Method did not intend to trivialise, infantilise or eroticise women.[93] Through several processes, however, the narrative on the body served as a tool to impose principles of sex differentiation and strict maintenance of the gender order.

The opposition between women's invisibility and men's visibility was the first principle upon which the text was based. Although the prologue announces that 'the French Method is applicable to all French people without any distinction of age and sex',[94] the implicit reference was man. The book, which was illustrated with more than 1100 photographs, only showed boys and men. The neutrality reached its limits, too, when considering the section on the physiological development of individuals. There the authors did not mention any example of a girl or woman; they nevertheless pointed out that young boys must be trained and that physical education could lead to military purposes. They also later referred to one of the most important goals of the method: the development of virility. Finally, among the 750 pages of the book two at least were especially dedicated to girls' physical education, suggesting possibly that the 748 other pages rather concerned boys and men. There was no need to write a section on boys' physical education, because the implicit norm to write about physical exercise and sports training was masculine.

Women were considered physically inferior to men, because 'their muscular power, measured with the lumbar dynamometer, represents only approximately two-thirds that of men'.[95] The statement referred to scientific knowledge in order to prove the natural and irrefutable character of the hierarchy between the sexes. In doing so, it opened the door to a process of essentialisation of the traits connoted

[91]Mary Louise Roberts, *Civilization without Sexes: Reconstructing Gender in Postwar France 1917–1927* (Chicago, IL: Chicago University Press 1994).

[92]Christine Bard, *Les garçonnes. Modes et fantasmes des Années folles* (Paris: Flammarion, 1998).

[93]Margaret C. Duncan and Michaël A Messner, 'The Media Image of Sport and Sex', in *MediaSport*, ed. L.A. Wenner (London: Routledge, 1998), 170–85; Thierry Terret, 'Sports and Erotica: Erotic Postcards of Sportswomen during France's *Années Folles*', *Journal of Sport History* 29, no. 2 (2002): 271–87.

[94]Ministère de la Guerre, *Règlement général d'éducation physique*, 5.

[95]Ministère de la Guerre, *Règlement général d'éducation physique*, 16.

as masculine or feminine. After puberty boys were said to look instinctively for occasions to produce extensive muscular efforts, whereas girls were supposed to remain on the contrary quiet and more reserved.[96] In presenting such stereotypes, the authors opposed weak, fragile, calm and docile women to valiant, strong, tough and courageous men, hence two different conceptions of physicality:

> Girls shall not look for exercises which require a certain development of strength. We shall thus not aim at developing the muscles of women and we shall be careful not to apply to them, without precaution, the forms of physical education reserved for young men…. Their physical education must be essentially hygienic. Intense efforts are not healthy for them: they tire them and, if prolonged, eventually damage irremediably their health.[97]

On the other hand, the authors expected physical education to develop health, strength, resistance, skilfulness, harmony of the body proportions and temperament in boys. They valued firmness and endurance, boldness and calmness, love of decision-making, fighting and responsibilities, all qualities supposed to constitute virility.[98]

The evocation of social roles in connection with the 'natural' characters of the sexes was a third way to fix the gender order. Girls were asked to prepare themselves for motherhood and marriage, whereas boys were ideally expected to become workers or soldiers. For girls:

> The special physiological functions which they have to fulfil and undergo are incompatible with intense heavy labour. When added to muscular fatigue, menstruation during adolescence, and pregnancy and baby feeding later result in exhaustion. Women are not built to fight but to procreate.[99]

For boys, physical education could help increase the output in professional, military or industrial positions.[100] Both sexes were asked to reach a certain level of accomplishment, but men were pushed towards achievement and frontiersmanship, in other words the outside world, whereas women had to focus on the inside world: the home.[101] This long-term division had a direct influence on the type of activities that were supposed to be more appropriate for men and women. For girls, exercises were expected to contribute to the development of the pelvis. Thus, walking, exercises of rhythmic and short-time suspension, jumping over a rope, discus and javelin throws, light shot-putt, racket sports (*paume*, tennis) and fencing with both arms were examples of recommended exercises. According to French sports historian

---

[96]Ministère de la Guerre, *Règlement général d'éducation physique*, 16.

[97]Ministère de la Guerre, *Règlement général d'éducation physique*, 16.

[98]Ministère de la Guerre, *Règlement général d'éducation physique*, 21.

[99]Ministère de la Guerre, *Règlement général d'éducation physique*, 16.

[100]Ministère de la Guerre, *Règlement général d'éducation physique*, 17.

[101]Nick Trujillo, 'Hegemonic Masculinity on the Mound: Media Representations of Nolan Ryan and American Sports Culture', in *Reading Sport: Critical Essays on Power and Representation*, ed. Susan Birrell and Mary G. McDonald (Boston: Northeastern University Press, 2000), 14–39.

Jean-Michel Delaplace, physical education for girls was to some extent 'gynaecological'.[102] Conversely, boys and men could practise every kind of exercise, depending on their age and health status.

In defining the most appropriate and legitimate practices for each sex, the narrative also shaped the limits of illegitimacy and inappropriateness. In particular, girls and women had explicitly to avoid 'any exercise which comes along with clashes, shocks and knocks which are dangerous for the uterine organ'.[103] By contrast not a word was said about dancing for boys and men, at a time when dance was presented as typically appropriate for girls' educational purposes.

Heterosexuality was the final nexus of the gender order; it was constructed through social relationships among men and among women, and exclusive sexual relations between men and women. Whereas the French Method did not primarily focus on girls' behaviour, it gave more details on the hegemonic male sexuality which, among other aspects, required not being effeminate and thus acting and presenting oneself as a man.[104] Apart from the development of physical and moral qualities that were obviously associated with masculinity, the text mentions the need for a better 'harmony of the forms and proportions of the body', an idea which, at a first glance, could be perceived as ambiguous in terms of gender markers. It was not the case, however, because this harmony resulted from 'the integrity of the organs, a normal development of the muscles, a solid and symmetric skeleton without angles, and a flexible-like and firm attitude'.[105] Affirmation of manliness definitively appeared beyond the aesthetics project.

Conclusion

Historians looking at the French method of physical education have been first sensitive to its role in the institutional and pedagogic history of physical education. Their main conclusion was that the method had been able to put the 'war of methods' to an end and that it mirrored the need for peace and consensus which characterised the context of the post-war. Indeed in the aftermath of the First World War, the French National Assembly rallied round the electoral alliance of right-wing and centre parties with the aim of putting forward a reconstruction plan for France. 'Winning the peace' appeared all the more difficult since military victory had been won at the expense of great sacrifice, and parliamentary debates still oscillated between tradition and modernity.[106] In the 1920s, players in the field of French physical education were also preparing to respond to the vulnerability of the French population. Whether in the case of ensuring the social integration of *Poilus* injured in the fighting or that of French women whose social condition was once more being ques-

---

[102]Jean-Michel Delaplace, 'Conception de l'éducation physique féminine en France entre les deux guerres: vers une gymnastique gynécologique?', in *Histoire du sport féminin*, ed. Pierre Arnaud and Thierry Terret (Paris: L'Harmattan, 1996, vol. 2), 69–79.

[103]Ministère de la Guerre, *Règlement général d'éducation physique*, 17.

[104]Gregory M. Herek. 'On Heterosexual Masculinity: Some Psychical Consequences of the Social Construction of Gender and Sexuality', in *Changing Men: New Directions in Research on Men and Masculinity*, ed. Michael S. Kimmel (Newbury Park, CA: Sage, 1987), 68–82.

[105]Ministère de la Guerre, *Règlement général d'éducation physique*, 21.

[106]Jean-Baptiste Duroselle, *Clemenceau* (Paris, Fayard, 1988); Jean-Jacques Becker and Serge Berstein, *Victoire et frustration* (Paris, Seuil, 1990).

tioned despite the Great War having given them an opportunity to demonstrate their social status, or then again in the case of France's youth suffering from a moral crisis that the Republican school strove to contain, each one was seeking a consensual solution. The French method of physical education from Joinville undoubtedly aspired to achieve social peace, while pursuing unquestionably geopolitical challenges. Yet although historiography long concerned itself with the former, alongside the method's pedagogic limits, while emphasising more the aspect of continuity in the case of Joinville's policy than that of rupture, more recent works have shown, by cross-referencing perspectives in the history of methods with those of France's social, political and cultural history in the 1920s, that this massive programme reflected something more than an ambitious project of building bodies. These later works were nourished by the cultural history of politics, the history of international relations and, more topically, by both gender studies and colonial studies. They also benefited from several monographs on the history of sport during the 1920s where the French method was systematically mentioned, although often incidentally. In so doing, they put the method in a wider context and made visible its more complex social and political significance. Thanks to a more deconstructionist approach to history, however, it would be important to better distinguish the different parts constituting the three volumes of the method. Indeed there is little doubt that several authors, including scientists, military personnel, educators and trainers, took part in the process of writing. As long as their names are unknown it remains difficult to fully understand the many levels on which there was interference during publication.

Yet the French method formed part of the context of reconstruction of nations and rethinking of relationships between states. From this point of view, it could be analysed as a political project resolutely turned both towards and away from the nation, as had already been the case previously in other countries.[107] On the one hand, it solidified the sociocultural foundations of defensive French nationalism by imposing a model of body, gender and race on the whole of the French population in the aftermath of the war that had shaken them. On the other, it contributed to displaying France's place on the international educational and sporting scene. In this way, the French method played a part in promoting French know-how and prestige, not only in the face of yesterday's enemies, but also as a response to the new imperial, political and economic rivalries of its allies. In this sense, the French method undoubtedly showed France's insecurities and ambitions in the new world order resulting from four years' dreadful warfare which had weakened the country's social norms and caused it to lose its status as great power. Thanks to this sudden burst of national pride, the French method of physical education enjoyed a long institutional life since it continued, at least officially, to be recommended in French military and school systems until the end of the 1960s.

---

[107]The combination of internal political use and exportation of national models and methods of gymnastics was especially strong in the period of nation-making during the nineteenth century. Among several examples, the case of the German *Turnen* is probably the best known. See for instance Michael Krüger, 'Body Culture and Nation Building: The History of Gymnastics in Germany in the Period of its Foundation as a Nation-state', *International Journal of the History of Sport* 13, no. 3 (1996): 409-417; Annette R. Hofmann, *Turnen and Sport: Transatlantic Transfers* (Münster: Waxmann, 2004).

Physical education for citizenship or humanity? Freethinkers and natural education in the Netherlands in the mid-nineteenth century

Vincent Stolk, Willeke Los and Wiel Veugelers

J.P. van Praag Institute, University of Humanistic Studies, Utrecht, The Netherlands

Studies in the history of physical education show that it was often promoted for socio-political reasons: to stimulate nation-building or increase economic productivity and/or military strength. By contrast, a different kind of motivation has received little attention in historical studies: the importance of physical education for the perfection of the individual, as expressed by the German neohumanistic word 'Bildung'. This article presents a case study in which the debate on the importance of physical education in the Netherlands in the mid-nineteenth century is examined. Ideas on the importance of Bildung in physical education especially existed within the freethinkers' movement. With arguments derived from their naturalistic worldview, freethinkers contested educational approaches that obstructed the natural development of the child. This case study aims to contribute to a better insight into the history of physical education in the Netherlands and into the diversity of reasons for promoting physical education in the past.

Introduction

At least since Rousseau, it has been a fundamental question in the field of education as to whether children are primarily to be raised to become citizens or rather to develop into rounded human beings.[1] Several scholars working in the history of physical education have studied the various answers given to this question. In general, they have suggested that the answer most often given is 'citizens', since they emphasised the role played by the state or society in physical education. An example of this is when physical education is used as an instrument in nation-building: when the state tries to identify physical health with the 'health' of the nation, or more directly for nationalistic purposes, as was the case with the Turn movement in

---

[1]J.J. Rousseau, *Emile or On Education*, trans. Barbara Foxley (Sioux Falls: NuVision Publications, 2007), 13.

early nineteenth-century Germany.[2] Another example is the use of physical education as a means of stimulating the productivity of working men and women, as was the case in the Soviet Union.[3] Probably the most convincing example, however, is when the state stimulates physical education for military purposes.[4] It is typical that the first national organisation for sport education in the Netherlands taught 'education in weaponry' besides gymnastics and made children do fencing exercises.[5] All these examples indicate that physical education in schools is often used for, as Miklos Hadas called it, the 'corporeal foundation of the modern state'.[6] This kind of research is in line with the work of Michel Foucault on disciplining the body. Foucault shows how society tries to regulate and discipline the body. Education played and still plays an important role in regulating the body and identity to adapt to the needs of society.[7]

In this article, we focus on a different kind of motivation for physical education, one that has been less researched by historians: the perfection of the individual person, the education aimed at the attainment of full humanity, as expressed by the

---

[2]Michael Krüger, 'Body Culture and Nation Building: The History of Gymnastics in Germany in the Period of its Foundation as a Nation-State', *International Journal of the History of Sport* 13, no. 3 (1996): 409–17. For other examples concerning Turkey, Hungary, Serbia and Greece, see Cüneyd Okay, 'Sport and Nation Building: Gymnastics and Sport in the Ottoman State and the Committee of Union and Progress, 1908–18', *International Journal of the History of Sport* 20, no. 1 (2003): 152–6; Miklos Hadas, 'The Rationalisation of the Body: Physical Education in Hungary in the Nineteenth Century', *History of Education* 38, no. 1 (2009): 61–78; Dusan Vuksanovic, 'Exercising for the Future: Nationalistic Ideas as Factors in Gymnastics Implementation in the 1860s Serbian Primary School System' (paper presented at the History of Education Society (HES) annual conference, Glasgow, Scotland, 25–27 November 2011 – henceforth, HES conference 2011); Dimitrios Foreinos, 'Images of the Body: Moulding the Political Soul – the Greek Gymnastics Curriculum from the Post-War Era (1950) to the Olympic Games of Athens (2004) and beyond (2008)' (paper presented at the HES conference 2011).

[3]Alison Rowley, 'Sport in the Service of the State: Images of Physical Culture and Soviet Women', *International Journal of the History of Sport* 23, no. 8 (2006): 1314–40. For other examples concerning Malaya and France, see Janice N. Brownfoot, '"Healthy Bodies, Healthy Minds": Sport and Society in Colonial Malaya', *International Journal of the History of Sport* 19, no. 2–3 (2002): 129–56; J. Gleyse and others, 'Physical Education as a Subject in France (School Curriculum, Policies and Discourse): The Body and the Metaphors of the Engine – Elements used in the Analyses of a Power and Control System during the Second Industrial Revolution', *Sport, Education and Society* 7, no. 1 (2002): 5–23.

[4]See, for example, J. A. Mangan and Frank Galligan, 'Militarism, Drill and Elementary Education: Birmingham Nonconformist Responses to Conformist Responses to the Teutonic Threat Prior to the Great War', *International Journal of the History of Sport* 28, no. 3 (2011): 568–604; David Kirk and Karen Twigg, 'The Militarization of School Physical Training in Australia: The Rise and Demise of the Junior Cadet Training Scheme, 1911–1931', *History of Education* 22, no. 4 (1993): 391–414; Marcel Spivak, *Les Origines Militaires De l'Education Physique En France, 1774–1848* (Paris: Ministère d'Etat, 1972).

[5]Leo Staal, *Een leeuw van honderd: Facetten van de turnbeweging in Nederland belicht t.g. v. het eeuwfeest van het Koninklijk Nederlands Gymnastiek Verbond, 15 maart 1868–1968* (Leiden: Meander, 1968), 12.

[6]'"Sound Mind in a Sound Body": Sports, Education, and Masculinities in Early Nineteenth-Century Hungary' (paper presented at the HES conference 2011).

[7]Michel Foucault, *Discipline and Punish* (New York: Vintage Books, 1979); Stephen Ball, ed., *Foucault and Education: Disciplines and Knowledge* (New York: Routledge, 1990); Gail McNail Jardine, *Foucault & Education* (New York: Peter Lang, 2005).

German neohumanistic term 'Bildung'.[8] Although the concept of Bildung is usually applied to cultural and intellectual education, Wilhelm von Humboldt (1767–1835), a key figure in the neohumanistic educational tradition, also stressed the inclusion of physical education in the education towards perfection.[9] By using the perspective of Bildung, we hope to contribute to a better understanding of the diversity of reasons why people in the past advocated physical education.

We approach this topic by presenting a case study: the physical education of young children (up to the primary school age of 12) in the Netherlands in the mid-nineteenth century. A modern primary school system in the Netherlands was established in 1806. Physical education, however, was not included in the curriculum. From the 1820s onwards it was debated whether or not this should be done. The debate reached a peak in the 1840s and 1850s, leading up to the revision of the 1857 primary school law, in which physical education was included in the curriculum as the optional school subject 'gymnastics'. In this article, we focus on the two main contributors to this debate, the teacher R.G. Rijkens (1795–1855) and the German educationist Carl Euler (1809–1882), in order to discuss the leading socio-political arguments for the acceptance of physical education. Furthermore, we focus on S.P. Scheltema (1801–1873), a physician who also participated in the debate about physical education.[10] He committed himself to De Dageraad (the Dawn), a journal established in 1855 by freethinkers: a group of lower middle-class, non-dogmatic thinkers who challenged the Church and orthodox Christian thinking.

Because of the importance given to the freethinkers' movement in this article, it is first necessary to supply some background information. In general, the freethinkers' movement in the Netherlands was relatively small, reaching a maximum of one thousand members in the nineteenth century. The freethinkers' organisation De Dageraad, the first and main Dutch freethinkers' organisation, was established in 1856 by members of the Amsterdam dissident freemasons' lodge 'Post Nubila Lux'

---

[8]Daniël Lechner, *"Bildung Macht Frei!": Humanistische en realistische vorming in Duitsland 1600–1860* (Amsterdam: Aksant, 2003), ix–xii; Hilda Amsing, *Bakens verzetten in het voortgezet onderwijs, 1863–1920: Gymnasium, h.b.s. en m.m.s. in onderwijssysteem, leerplan en geschiedenisonderwijs* (Delft: Eburon, 2002), 24; Ludwig Fertig, *Zeitgeist und Erziehungskunst: Eine Einführung in die Kulturgeschichte der Erziehung in Deutschland von 1600 bis 1900* (Darmstadt: Wissenschaftliche Buchgesellschaft, 1984), 297–8.

[9]Torsten Schmidt-millard, 'Perspectives of Modern Sports Pedagogy', *European Journal of Sport Science* 3, no. 3 (2003): 2; Felix Saure, 'Beautiful Bodies, Exercising Warriors and Original Peoples: Sports, Greek Antiquity and National Identity from Winckelmann to "Turnvater Jahn"', *German History* 27, no. 3 (2009): 358–73. See, for Plato, one of Humboldt's sources of inspiration, on physical education, Werner Jaeger, *Paideia. Die Formung des Griechischen Menschen*, vol. 2, 3rd ed. (Berlin 1959), 306–10.

[10]S.P. Scheltema, *Over den invloed van het gevoel voor het schoone op de zedelijke volmaking des menschen*, 2nd ed. (Arnhem: G. van Eldik Thieme, 1849); S.P. Scheltema, *Over opvoeding en het behoud van kinderlijken zin* (Amsterdam: Johannes Müller, 1842); S.P. Scheltema, *Over het nut van de gymnastische oefeningen voor ligchaam en geest* (Arnhem: Stenfert Kroese, 1851).

LIVERPOOL JOHN MOORES UNIVERSITY
LEARNING SERVICES

(Beyond the Clouds, the Light), in the Netherlands.[11] De Dageraad was modest in size compared with freethinkers' organisations in neighbouring countries such as England, Germany, Belgium and France. This difference can be explained by the fact that the leading Protestant church in the Netherlands, the 'Nederlandsche Hervormde Kerk' (the Dutch Reformed Church), was not a privileged 'state church', and had a smaller grasp on society compared with other West European countries. The Roman Catholics, about 35 percent of the Dutch population around 1850, had an even weaker position in the Netherlands. The effect of the relatively weak position of the Church on the influence of the Dutch freethinkers can be illustrated by a comparison between the Dutch and the Belgian and French educational systems. In the Netherlands, education was largely a state matter, while in Belgium and France the clergy were highly influential in educational matters. Consequently, Dutch freethinkers had less need to organise themselves in order to challenge the Church in this specific area.[12]

This is not to say that the freethinkers in the Netherlands had no reason to exist. Even though the Church and the state were officially separated during the nineteenth century, Christianity was still omnipresent in Dutch society. Therefore, freethinkers still found it necessary to challenge the Church's epistemological claims and its direct or indirect influence in several areas of social life (among them education and poor relief). They were successful in this in at least three ways. First, freethinkers popularised scientific knowledge for a wider audience, especially for members of the working class, stimulating them to question ecclesiastical authority and leave the church. Second, especially since the latter decades of the nineteenth century, freethinkers played leading parts in social reform movements, including feminism and the campaigns for cremation and sexual reform. Third, in line with the previous point, influential social reformers like Multatuli (pseudonym of Eduard Douwes Dekker, 1820–1887), Ferdinand Domela Nieuwenhuis (1846–1919) and Aletta Jacobs (1854–1929) were for a longer or shorter time part of the freethinkers' movement. For them, De Dageraad functioned at least in some sense as an educational institute and social meeting place.[13]

Since we are focusing on the debate on physical education in the mid-nineteenth century, we are dealing with the freethinkers' movement in the first phase of its existence. Although freethinkers in this period were not primarily interested in

---

[11]Because the freethinkers' movement originated from a *dissident* freemasons' lodge, and there were no formal ties between lodges and the freethinkers' movement, freemasonry and freethinking in the Netherlands must be seen as separate movements. The Dutch freethinkers started as a movement with its own goals, partly because they found freemasonry too introverted and too ritualised. See also Vincent Stolk, *De dageraad van het positief atheïsme. Jan Hoving over godsdienst en seksualiteit in het Interbellum* (Breda 2006), 37–8. In France, the ties between freemasonry and freethinking were much stronger, while in England and Germany the relationship was absent.

[12]J.G.A. ten Bokkel, *Gidsen en genieën. De Dageraad en het vrije denken in Nederland 1855–1898* (Dieren: FAMA Maçonnieke Uitgeverij, 2003), 159–76; H. Moors, 'Helpt vrijdenken? Vrijdenkersorganisaties in negentiende-eeuws Nederland en België: naar een comparatieve benadering', *Brood & Rozen. Tijdschrift voor de geschiedenis van sociale bewegingen* 3, no. 2 (1998): 13–29.

[13]H. Moors, 'Bijbels en boenwas. Over de plaats van de vrijdenkersbeweging in negentiende-eeuws Nederland', *Kleio* 42, no. 6 (2001): 12–13; J.H.C. Blom, 'De vrijdenkersbeweging in Nederland. Enkele inleidende opmerkingen', in *God noch autoriteit: Geschiedenis van de vrijdenkersbeweging in Nederland*, ed. B. Gasenbeek, J.C.H. Blom and J.W.M. Nabuurs (Amsterdam: Boom, 2006), 11–24; Ten Bokkel, *Gidsen en genieën*, 128–30.

pedagogy and the school system, they did apply their nonconformist philosophical and natural-theological ideas to the field of (physical) education.[14] This meant that – although many freethinkers were also primary school teachers – they looked at physical education from a different angle from leading writers such as Rijkens and Euler, whose main concern was education. By focusing on what Scheltema and other important freethinkers, such as the physician Franz Wilhelm Junghuhn (1809–1864) and Multatuli, wrote on physical education, we shall try to show that their involvement in the freethinkers' movement explains why humanity and individual development, and not the interests of the state, were their main objectives in (physical) education.

The origins of gymnastics in the Netherlands

Before physical education was included as an optional subject in the curriculum for primary schools in 1857, and even made compulsory in the secondary schools in 1863, there had been much debate on the possible benefits or disadvantages of the subject. An organisation that became an advocate for physical education in schools was the 'Maatschappij tot Nut van 't Algemeen' (Society for Public Welfare, here: the Society). It was founded in 1784 in a patriotic, enlightened environment and contributed to the creation of a centralised educational system in the Netherlands in 1806, as part of the Batavian Revolution.[15] The Society was then, apparently, not yet fully convinced of the usefulness of physical education, did not yet know enough of it, or found it too expensive or impractical to make it a part of the school system.[16]

This changed during the first half of the nineteenth century. Especially after 1840, the Society actively advocated physical education in schools. Among other things, it issued a prize contest for the best practical guide for physical exercises in 1842 and petitioned the king in 1849, shortly after the constitutional revision of 1848, to make physical education in school compulsory by law. When the petition turned out to be ineffective, the Society established schools for gymnastics in several cities (e.g. Amsterdam, Rotterdam and Groningen) in the 1850s. These schools

---

[14]Tom Steele, *Knowledge is Power! The Rise and Fall of European Popular Educational Movements, 1848–1939* (Oxford: Lang, 2007). Steele writes: 'Educational reform and the radical revaluation of sources of knowledge or epistemology really go hand in hand' (p. 6). This explains why freethinkers, who indeed challenged authoritative sources of knowledge such as the Bible, became interested in education and even hoped (but failed) to establish their own freethinkers' university and schools for primary education, see 'Verslag der vergadering, gehouden op het jaarfeest der vereeniging' (unpublished report, 1857); 2.0.2. Archive Vrijdenkersvereniging 'De Dageraad', International Institute for Social History, Amsterdam (henceforth, IISH).

[15]See for this history earlier articles by B.J. Hake in this journal: 'The Making of Batavian Citizens: Social Organisation of Constitutional Enlightenment in The Netherlands, 1795–98', 23, no. 4 (1994): 335–53; 'The Pedagogy of *Useful Knowledge For The Common Man*: The Lending Libraries of the Society for the Common Benefit in The Netherlands, 1794–1813', 29, no. 6 (2000): 495–515.

[16]J.P. Kramer and Niels Lommen, *Geschiedenis van de lichamelijke opvoeding in Nederland* (Meppel: Ten Brink, 1987), 26–7.

were meant to demonstrate the value of gymnastics and to stimulate teacher apprentices to experiment with it in their own schools.[17]

The Society was not the only one supporting the case of physical education. From the beginning of the nineteenth century several theologians and teachers had been writing about the subject. The most influential were R.G. Rijkens (1795–1855) and Carl Euler (1809–1882).[18] Rijkens was a school headmaster in a small town called Onnen, near Groningen, and was the first in the Netherlands to work with gymnastic equipment in a school. In 1843 he wrote a voluminous book about gymnastics that became widely known.[19] This book made the Society withdraw its aforementioned prize contest for the best practical guide: Rijkens's book, besides containing hundreds of pages devoted to the theory of gymnastics, also supplied the practical need. The fame of the book was stimulated by the fact that the Society sent it to all its approximately 250 local departments.[20]

The German Euler, 'the famous Turner' as he was known in the Netherlands, was also an influential person in the field of physical education. He had left his country because of his involvement in the revolutionary movement in the late 1840s, when leaders of 'Turnvereine' (sport clubs) were often involved in revolutionary nationalistic groups.[21] Despite this background, Euler was appointed as a sports teacher at the Teacher Training College in Haarlem in 1851, which was originally set up by the Society, but was taken over by the state in 1816. He stayed in the Netherlands until 1860 when he moved to Belgium. His best-known book about gymnastics, *De Gymnastiek en hare invoering in Nederland* (Gymnastics and its Implementation in the Netherlands) was published in 1853.[22]

Body and mind

Euler and, especially, Rijkens used one key argument for the promotion of gymnastics: ever since the introduction of the school law of 1806 teaching had focused too much on knowledge transmission. Children were overloaded with scientific

---

[17]W.W. Mijnhardt and A.J. Wichers, *Om het algemeen volksgeluk. Twee eeuwen particulier initiatief 1784–1984. Gedenkboek ter gelegenheid van het tweehonderdjarig bestaan van de Maatschappij tot Nut van 't algemeen* (Edam: Maatschappij tot Nut van 't Algemeen, 1984), 49–51; *Jaarboek der Maatschappij tot Nut van 't Algemeen voor 1854–1855* (Amsterdam: C.A. Spin & Zoon, 1856), 50.

[18]Kramer and Lommen, *Lichamelijke opvoeding*, 21–5.

[19]R.G. Rijkens, *Praktische handleiding voor kunstmatige ligchaams-oefeningen, ten dienste van huisgezinnen en verschillende inrigtingen voor onderwijs en opvoeding; bevattende mede eenige vrijmoedige gedachten over de hedendaagsche opvoeding, en eene menigte oefeningen ter vóórkoming en wegneming van verschillende ligchaamsgebreken* (Groningen: J. Oomkens, 1843).

[20]Carl Euler, '"Gymnastiek" door R.G. Rijkens', *De Gids* 21, no. 1 (1857): 863–71; Anon., 'R.G. Rijkens', *Nieuw Nederlandsch tijdschrift voor onderwijs en opvoeding* 1 (1855): 65–72; Mijnhardt and Wichers, *Algemeen volksgeluk*, 49–51.

[21]For more about this and bibliographic references, see Krüger, 'Body Culture'. Euler is called a famous Turner in G.E.V.S., '*Schat der gezondheid*, een tijdschrift voor alle standen, tot bevordering van volkswelvaart, door verspreiding van eenvoudige beginselen van gezondheidsleer en openbare gezondheidsregeling, en hunne toepassing op het individueel en maatschappelijk leven', *De Gids* 25 (1861): 525.

[22]P. Delheye, 'Carl Euler (1809–1882): Een Duitse turnapologeet in Brussel', *Sportimonium*, no. 2 (2001): 25–33.

information, or at least information that would be useful for the scientific or economic development of the Netherlands. At the same time, moral education had a central position in Dutch school law. According to leading Dutch historians of education, moralising and socialising were in fact the main tasks of teachers.[23]

Intellectual and moral development were thus provided for in primary schools, whereas the body was neglected. Against this, Rijkens and Euler argued that body and mind were not separate entities. According to them, the interconnectedness of body and mind explained why children who were only intellectually and morally developed, while their physical development was neglected, most of the time were weak, prone to diseases and useless – even immoral, because the energy that was not let out by exercising would persuade the child to commit the sin of Onan. Only by harmoniously developing both body and mind could a child become a moral and valuable member of society.[24]

This holistic view of man had its source in antiquity ('mens sana in corpore sano') and was widespread throughout Europe.[25] The German scholar Felix Saure writes that well-known German writers on physical education were inspired by the body culture of the ancient Greeks and took over their ideas regarding the symbiotic relationship between body and mind. Just as the Greeks had not separated intellectual from physical education in the public sphere, for instance in schools, so too the German educator did not divide what nature had united.[26]

Euler, himself a German, used the body–mind rhetoric as the opening argument in his 1853 book. Just as the Germans were doing under the guidance of 'Turnvater' Friedrich Ludwig Jahn (1778–1852), the Dutch should restore the broken wholeness in education by giving gymnastics the place it deserved.[27] Rijkens, who used almost without exception German sources in both his books about gymnastics, used the body–mind rhetoric many times.[28] The role of antiquity played an explicit role in this discourse, as he wrote: 'The ancients already said that the only way to preserve soul and body is not to exercise the soul without the body, nor the body without the soul, so that by mutual help they remain balanced and healthy.'[29]

---

[23]Nelleke Bakker, *Kind en karakter: Nederlandse pedagogen over opvoeding in het gezin 1845–1925* (Amsterdam: Het Spinhuis, 1995), 6; Ernst Mulder, 'Arbeid en onderwijs. "Beroepsbekwaamheid" en "beroepszedelijkheid" in de negentiende en twintigste eeuw', in *Geschiedenis van opvoeding en onderwijs. Inleiding, bronnen, onderzoek*, eds. Bernard Kruithof, Jan Noordman and Piet de Rooy (Nijmegen: SUN, 1982), 353–4; Boudien de Vries, 'De waarde van kennis bij arbeiders en de kleine burgerij in de tweede helft van de negentiende eeuw', *De Negentiende Eeuw* 33, no. 1 (2009): 53–70; Jeroen J. H. Dekker, *Het verlangen naar opvoeden: Over de groei van de pedagogische ruimte in Nederland sinds de Gouden Eeuw tot omstreeks 1900* (Amsterdam: Bakker, 2006), 187–90.

[24]Euler, *De gymnastiek*, 2; Rijkens, *Praktische handleiding*, e.g. i–viii, xxviii–xxix.

[25]This was put forward in several papers presented at the HES conference 2011, for example: Foreinos, 'Images of the Body'; Hadas, 'Sound Mind'; Jackie Farr, '*A Sound Mind in a Sound Body*: Dartford College of Physical Education and the Bergman Österberg Archive'.

[26]Saure, 'Beautiful Bodies'.

[27]Euler, *De gymnastiek*, 2–6.

[28]R.G. Rijkens, *Gymnastie* (Amsterdam: Weytingh & Van der Haart, 1855); Rijkens, *Praktische handleiding*.

[29]Rijkens, *Praktische handleiding*, 1.

The purpose of physical education

Arguing that bodily development was at least as important as intellectual education did not yet answer the question of to what purpose physical education should be promoted. Saure writes that leading German *Turners*, such as G.U.A. Vieth (1763–1836) und J.C.F. GutsMuths (1759–1839), shared the ideas of the Philanthropists, the eighteenth-century German reformers who applied enlightened ideas to the field of education. Philanthropists believed in human enhancement through education and aimed at raising enlightened and useful citizens of the state. The latter was clearly their main objective: the improvement of the state, or the social dimension of physical education, was valued more highly than the individual dimension, the well-being of a single person.[30]

We recognise this objective in the promotion of physical education in the Netherlands. The Society was rooted in the Enlightenment and shared some of the important ideas of the Philanthropists. By means of (physical) education, the Society wanted to stimulate children from the lower social classes to grow up as strong and useful citizens who could make valuable contributions to the progress of the state, an effort that was part of the so-called 'bourgeois civilising offensive'.[31]

This motivation is present in Euler's work. He distinguished three goals of gymnastics. The first was the improvement of physical health. The second was character formation: the promotion of diligence, self-control, discipline and obedience, important social virtues that were often mentioned in respect of physical education. The third goal was the strength of the nation. Euler recognised that the Prussians were more preoccupied with militarism than the Dutch, but he nevertheless saw the potential benefits of physical education for Dutch workers who – as he thought was generally accepted – were less productive than those in Germany and England. And as the well-known physician Herman van Cappelle (1825–1890) commented on Euler's work, physical education could have beneficial effects on the Dutch soldiers who fought the colonial wars in the East Indies.[32]

How Rijkens thought of the function of physical education is illustrated by this comment at the end of the introduction to his magnum opus:

> We wish to educate well-behaving subjects of the state, who love their country, honour the government, obey the laws and seek happiness in loyally fulfilling their duty

---

[30]Saure, 'Beautiful Bodies', 361–4. See also Jan Lenders, 'Van kind tot burger. Lager onderwijs en de vorming tot burgerschap in de negentiende eeuw', in *Tot burgerschap en deugd: Volksopvoeding in de negentiende eeuw*, ed. Nelleke Bakker and Rudolf Dekker (Hilversum: Verloren, 2006), 14–15; Bernard Kruithof, '"Godsvrucht en goede zeden bevorderen". Het burgerlijk beschavingsoffensief van de Maatschappij tot Nut van 't Algemeen', in *Tot burgerschap en deugd*, 69–79; Kruithof, *Zonde en deugd in domineesland: Nederlandse protestanten en problemen van opvoeding: zeventiende tot twintigste eeuw* (Groningen: Wolters-Noordhoff, 1990), 16; A.W.M. Duijx, *De filantropijnen: Bibliografie van de in Nederland aanwezige boeken van J.B. Basedow, J.H. Campe en Chr.G. Salzmann* (Leiden: Subfakulteit der Pedagogische en Andragogische Wetenschappen, Rijksuniversiteit Leiden, 1985), 1–4.

[31]Ivo van Hilvoorde, 'Fitness: The Early (Dutch) Roots of a Modern Industry', *International Journal of the History of Sport* 25, no. 10 (2008): 1309; Kruithof, 'Godsvrucht en goede zeden', 69–79.

[32]Euler, *De gymnastiek*, 6–66; H. van Cappelle, 'De gymnastiek en hare invoering in Nederland, door Carl Euler', *De Gids* 17 (1853): 741.

towards themselves, their fellow men and the Supreme Being; we want to make the physical and intellectual education serve that purpose.[33]

Under the heading 'gymnastics stimulates the education of good citizens' he made it clear that he was thinking especially of the lower classes, who would provide most of the workers in society: physical education would make them strong and industrious, preventing them from becoming lazy and poor – an argument that fitted well with the Philanthropic discourse. Rijkens did not repudiate individual happiness, but saw the use of physical education foremost in social terms.[34]

F.W. Junghuhn, nature and the place of physical education within freethought

Besides the social benefits of physical education, there also existed a different kind of answer to the question 'to what purpose?': physical education for the general development of the individual towards human perfection, expressed by the word 'Bildung'. Saure illustrates this by discussing Wilhelm von Humboldt and several German writers who were part of the Romantic Movement.[35] In the Netherlands, we see the same thing among freethinkers.

As we remarked in the introduction, freethinkers opposed the Church. But that did not make them atheists. Instead, they devoted themselves to 'natural religion and morality'. In this worldview, 'nature' was a core concept. As they used it in their journal *De Dageraad*, it could just mean 'physical nature', the object of natural science, but also nature as what is true and undisturbed by man, much like Rousseau's 'Nature within us', as opposed to society outside us.[36] The meanings that freethinkers gave to nature as an epistemological and moral concept were not common. Although the concept of nature as the source of true knowledge was shared by many contemporaries, freethinkers went further by valuing nature as the only source of true knowledge. The Bible, whether or not taken literally, was seen by non-freethinkers as the main guide for morality, while freethinkers esteemed nature as the highest source of morality.

How the natural religion and morality relates to physical education can be explained by focusing on the man who became the founder of the *De Dageraad*: the Dutch-Prussian physician, natural scientist and freemason F.W. Junghuhn. Junghuhn was well known because of his scientific investigations in the Dutch East Indies. He also wrote a book about religion and culture in Java, which was, like most of his work, published in Dutch (1854 and 1855) and German (1855). This book, *Licht- en schaduwbeelden uit de binnenlanden van Java* (Light and Shadow Images from the Inlands of Java) became the Bible of the Dutch freethinkers in the first decades of their existence. In *Licht- en schaduwbeelden* Junghuhn praised the people of Java for staying true to nature and criticised the Dutch for being spiritually as flattened out as their landscape. This made him highly critical of the Dutch attempts to convert the people of Java to Christianity. He promoted a deistic

---

[33]Rijkens, *Praktische handleiding*, xxxvii.

[34]Ibid., section D.

[35]Saure, 'Beautiful Bodies', 364–8.

[36]Rousseau, *Emile*, 13. In *De Dageraad*, this meaning of nature appeared in several articles on the human body, natural science, education, morality and supranaturalistic claims of Christianity.

worldview, which was truer to nature and therefore superior to orthodox Christianity. Especially because of this position, Junghuhn's reviewers rejected his book. This, however, could not prevent the appearance of another six editions in approximately the next 10 years, which suggests that people were both critical of and interested in Junghuhn's ideas.[37]

In the 'Gospel of Natural Religion and Morality', a part of his *Licht- en schaduwbeelden*, Junghuhn set out to explain his worldview. He described the two pillars of education as part of the system of natural religion. The first was mathematical and scientific education. If pupils were taught that the investigation of nature was a better source of knowledge than the supposed revelations of God, orthodox Christianity – an artificial, man-made religion according to Junghuhn – would soon lose its hegemony and automatically disappear. The second pillar was the 'strong development of a healthy body'. Junghuhn wrote that if the body of a person was damaged, his spirit would be too. And the other way round: a melancholic attitude would be accompanied by a weak constitution. In his vision, all nature was animated, a part of God, and so too was the human body. He even used religious terminology to describe mistreatment of the body; he saw taking insufficient rest and bad nourishment as acts of sin. Preachers of ascetics did exactly the opposite of what people ought to do: to honour God by honouring the body.[38]

According to Junghuhn, the natural and healthy development of the body should be stimulated from the moment a child was born; there should be no delay. This was the task of the mother, the natural caretaker of the child. At the age of approximately six, it became the task of the school. In Junghuhn's view, every school had to be an institution for physical exercises, not unlike the schools for gymnastics created by the Society, although Junghuhn did not mention them. He wrote that children should have the opportunity to walk, jump, climb, wrestle, swim, ride horses and do numerous other sports during school hours. Intellectual education, in the shape of the study of nature, was for Junghuhn and many other freethinkers an important task for schools, but this should be done in harmony with the child's own nature, by giving it the opportunity to exercise.[39]

As distinct from the Society and other Philanthropists, Junghuhn's aim with physical education was not social welfare, but individual happiness. Enjoying life was not just a right, but a duty imposed by the Creator.[40] And because bodily health was a precondition for this, the child had to be developed physically well, in harmony with his or her spirit, as was commanded by nature and thus by God.

Just as Junghuhn's deistic worldview played a leading role in the freethinkers movement, so did his two pillars of education. In the first series of the freethinkers' journal *De Dageraad*, which appeared between 1855 and 1868, the articles on

---

[37]De gebroeders Dag en Nacht (pseudonym of F.W. Junghuhn), *Licht- en schaduwbeelden uit de binnenlanden van Java: Over het karakter, de mate van beschaving, de zeden en gebruiken der Javanen, over de invoering van het Christendom op Java, het bezigen van vrijen arbeid en andere vragen van den dag* (Leiden: Hazenberg Corns. zoon; Amsterdam: Günst, 1854–1855). For the reception of this book, see Peter Sep, 'De receptie van licht- en schaduwbeelden uit de binnenlanden van Java van F.W. Junghuhn', *Indische letteren* 2, no. 2 (1987): 53–64.

[38]Junghuhn, *Licht- en schaduwbeelden*, 162–72.

[39]Ibid., 168–9.

[40]Ibid., 167.

physical education and body culture were in accordance with Junghuhn's ideas.[41] This was partly due to the fact that there existed a direct link between his *Licht- en schaduwbeelden* and *De Dageraad*. Junghuhn's book was thoroughly studied in the aforementioned freemasons' lodge Post Nubila Lux, of which Junghuhn and his publisher Frans Christiaan Günst (1823–1885) were both members. Several freemasons considered the lodge too narrow a platform to discuss and further develop Junghuhn's ideas on natural religion, so in 1855 they established a journal explicitly for this purpose. The name of the journal, *De Dageraad*, was the same as that of the freethinkers' organisation in Amsterdam created a year later. Günst, one of the founders of *De Dageraad*, became its publisher.[42]

S.P. Scheltema and natural education in *De Dageraad*

One of the early writers in the field of physical education, S.P. Scheltema, a medical practitioner in the town of Arnhem, one day noticed the cover of *De Dageraad* in a local bookstore. He soon came to admire the contributors for daring to tell the truth and after having contacted Günst he himself became involved as a writer for the journal and sometimes even acted on behalf of the editorial board.[43] Scheltema's background is interesting. Shortly after taking his PhD in 1833, he devoted himself to establishing a mental institution. He studied psychology, anthropology and philosophy in addition to his medical training in order to gain a better understanding of the mentally ill. The mental institution was never realised, but he used his acquired knowledge to publish on a wide variety of topics, such as religion, aestheticism (for which he won a prize contest of the Society in 1840),[44] moderation of alcohol use, and (physical) education.[45] One key thought reappeared in all his publications: the eminence of nature above culture.

His concept of 'natural education', which he borrowed from the German preacher and founder of boarding schools in the Netherlands, Friedrich Renatus Früauf (1764–1851), was central in his pedagogic and cultural thought.[46] 'Natural education', as explained by Früauf, was a non-artificial method of education that did not spoil the original character of the child or add alien elements to it. The goal was to ennoble every child, without separating it from its natural properties. This

---

[41]See especially Christophilus, 'Opvoeding', *De Dageraad* 4 (1857): 81–8, 161–72, 273–87, 369–91, 481–94; Simones, 'Opvoeding en onderwijs', *De Dageraad* 13 (1862): 52–69, 156–71, 249–60, 342–53; W. B. Westermann, 'Opvoeding en onderwijs', *De Dageraad* 21 (1866): 22–40, 90–100; Pope, 'Gezondheidsleer en opvoeding', *De Dageraad* 7 (1859): 47–62, 159–70.

[42]Siebe Thissen, *De Spinozisten: Wijsgerige beweging in Nederland (1850–1907)* (Den Haag: Sdu Uitgevers, 2000), 45–54; Ten Bokkel, *Gidsen en genieën*, 55–67.

[43]At least twice he answered letters that were addressed to the editorial board; see S.P. Scheltema, *Open antwoord van "De Dageraad", op den open brief van ds. A. G. van Anrooy, te Kampen* (Amsterdam: De Dageraad, 1857); Compassio (pseudonym of S.P. Scheltema), *Antwoord van Compassio aan Indignatio op zijn open brief aan De Dageraad* (Amsterdam: De Dageraad, 1858).

[44]S.P. Scheltema, *Over opvoeding*, 191.

[45]For Scheltema's background: 'Lijst van boekhandelaren' (unpublished document, 1868); 6.119. Archive Vrijdenkersvereniging 'De Dageraad', IISH; S.P. Scheltema, 'Open antwoord van dr. S.P. Scheltema, te Arnhem, op den open brief van pred. J.C.W. Quack, te Brakel', *De Dageraad* 10 (1860): 244–8.

[46]Scheltema, *Over opvoeding*, 80–1.

type of education was important to Scheltema, because he was highly critical of the achievements of Western society. Although it had become richer, more sophisticated and cultural, it had turned away from its natural roots. One aspect of this was that it had completely forgotten corporeality, as if the philosopher needed only his intelligence and the artist only his creativity. The growing numbers of mentally ill and languid people proved for Scheltema the overall deterioration of society and could be explained by the lack of physical education.[47]

An important cause of this was the fact that the individuality of people was sacrificed to their position as members of society. Scheltema complained that people were first of all seen as carpenters, cobblers and merchants, and only then, if at all, human beings. This made them perhaps useful, but only as members of a corrupt society.[48] He wrote:

> We see, how they [our children] are being educated as everything, except as human beings; how already in early youth they are designated and prepared for a position in society, but not for a position as man, in God's creation.[49]

Natural education was Scheltema's means of counteracting this. He wrote, in 1842, very much like Junghuhn would a decade later:

> As pedagogic elements must from now on be generally accepted: gymnastics and scientific education. They are as vital as writing and calculating, and to whatever rank of society someone belongs, whatever occupation they choose, always shall these two be indispensable for the education of human beings as human beings.[50]

Scheltema put his ideas on gymnastics into practice by buying equipment for physical exercises for his own son, but he also had higher goals. He promoted the concept of gymnastics by calling for new legislation and financially supporting initiatives in the area of physical education, like those of Rijkens and the Society. He also advocated better training of gymnastics teachers. Contemporary teachers' exams only tested knowledge related to subject content, but ignored what the apprentice knew about the physiological needs of children in different stages of their development.[51]

Scheltema also opposed the military drill instructors, who often became teachers at gymnastics schools.[52] They thought they knew everything about physical education, but in fact they harmed children by demanding too much of them. The same applied to sports teachers who tried to turn their pupils into acrobats and put them in danger by doing so, which was an objection commonly made against sports education in this period. In reply he referred to GutsMuths, who in 17 years of physical

---

[47]Scheltema, *De zedelijke volmaking*, 79; Scheltema, *Gymnastische oefeningen*, 11–14; Scheltema, 'Wat is beschaving of civilisatie?' *De Dageraad* 12 (1861): 1–12. Euler acknowledged the correlation between the highly populated mental institutions and the absence of physical education; see Euler, *De gymnastiek*, 20–42.

[48]Scheltema, *Gymnastische oefeningen*, 14–15, 23.

[49]Scheltema, *Over opvoeding*, 8. See also Scheltema, *Gymnastische oefeningen*, 14–16.

[50]Cited in Scheltema, *Gymnastische oefeningen*, 52.

[51]Ibid, 44–5, 55–6, 62.

[52]J.P. Kramer and C. van Reeth, 'Schets van de ontwikkeling van de lichamelijke opvoeding in Nederland', in *Het vergeten lichaam: geschiedenis van de lichamelijke opvoeding in België en Nederland*, eds. Mark D'Hoker and Jan Tolleneer (Leuven: Garant, 1995), 20–1.

education had never witnessed a single accident. Scheltema also opposed, just like Von Humboldt, competition as part of gymnastics. Using the body for winning a game instead of exercising it in a natural way obstructed the child's harmonious development. The key to proper physical education, according to Scheltema, was simply obeying the laws of nature.[53]

The above quotation also emphasises that physical education was intended for children, boys and girls, from all ranks of society. Scheltema thus stressed the ontological importance instead of the functional use of physical education. This differs from Rijkens and the Philanthropists who particularly had in mind the lower classes, from which working men came.

The professor and physician Jan van Geuns, whose uncle (also Jan van Geuns) was the translator of GutsMuths' famous book into Dutch, sympathised to a certain degree with Scheltema's ideas about natural education. He stressed, however, that when children reached adolescence they should start receiving cultural in addition to physical education in order to function properly in society.[54] This view expressed the same criticism that Rousseau had often received: his Émile would be of no use to society, just as Scheltema's children would if they received only natural education.

The ideas expressed in *Émile* were indeed similar to how freethinkers such as Scheltema thought about the relationship between education and society. Most of the people who were familiar with the contents of *Émile* appreciated Rousseau's pedagogic ideas, which they found child-friendly because they took individual peculiarities into account, but they rejected them on account of their practical uselessness: besides being unrealistic, Rousseau's views placed education wholly outside society. Scheltema wrote that although people no longer thought that Rousseau wished to raise 'bushmen or wild bears', they still preferred Pestalozzi to Rousseau, because 'Pestalozzi wanted to educate human beings, unlike Rousseau, without taking the social order into account, but by acknowledging that school and family educate people for society, that is: for home, state and church', as the headmaster D. de Groot, editor of the pedagogic journal *Pestalozzi*, wrote in 1869.[55]

In his writings in *De Dageraad*, Scheltema showed his more radical face and made it clear that according to De Groot's description he was more inclined to Rousseau than to Pestalozzi and did not agree with Van Geuns's critique. Freethinkers, because of their critical stance towards revealed religion, were banished to the margins of society anyway, so social acceptance was not their main concern. Scheltema admitted that a person educated in absolute accordance with nature would not always be found useful to society. That did not matter: in the long run, civilisation would be improved by healthy individuals who lived their lives in harmony with nature. Scheltema put it like this: 'Raising someone to be a member

---

[53]Scheltema, *Gymnastische oefeningen*, 30–3; Scheltema, *Over opvoeding*, 1–55.

[54]Jan van Geuns, 'Over opvoeding en het behoud van kinderlijken zin, door S.P. Scheltema', *De Gids* 1 (1844): 267–84.

[55]Scheltema, *Over opvoeding*, 80; D. de Groot, 'Bijdrage tot de beantwoording der vraag: hoe moet het wezen en het doel der opvoeding in onze dagen worden opgevat?', *Pestalozzi* 3 (1869): 157. Another well-known educator still thought that Rousseau wished to raise loveless Caribbean wild men; see A. van Otterloo, 'Redevoering, uitgesproken ter opening van de achttiende algemeene vergadering van het Nederlandsch Onderwijzers-Genootschap te Gorinchem, den 30 julij 1862', *Maandblad van het Nederlandsch Onderwijzers-Genootschap* 8, no. 10 (1862): 177–96.

of society is something different from raising someone to be an as-complete-as-possible man-type. The latter must be the goal.'[56]

Although (physical) education and bodily health were above all needed for the fulfilment of individual, natural needs, views like those of Scheltema were not in any sense antisocial. Freethinkers simply judged it unethical to raise a child to fit into a society they disapproved of. This reveals the peculiarity of the freethinkers when it comes to physical education: instead of using physical education to improve existing society, they used it for human enhancement, which they expected would eventually change society in more fundamental ways.

Multatuli

Throughout the first series of *De Dageraad* other freethinkers wrote in the same spirit, almost without exception pleading for education aimed at human perfection and pointing out to educators that they should understand the body and the physical demands of the child, so as to be able to support the child in a healthy lifestyle.[57]

But the impact of *De Dageraad* was limited. It had only a few hundred subscribers.[58] And although the journal was available throughout the country and everybody in the Netherlands knew of it, this acquaintance was highly superficial: freethinkers were against religion and therefore a moral threat to the nation, and that was about all that most people knew of them – with the exception, of course, of a loyal group of readers chiefly in Amsterdam, who were sympathetic towards or themselves members of *De Dageraad*, also situated in Amsterdam.[59]

There was, however, one freethinker who succeeded surprisingly well in becoming a popular spokesman for freethought. This was Eduard Douwes Dekker, better known as Multatuli, who was as critical of religion as he was of colonialism, for which he is most famous. In fact, his critique on religion and colonialism, as well as his critique on education and many other aspects of society, was all part of his general critical attitude towards Dutch culture, especially focusing on dishonesty, selfishness and petty-bourgeois narrow-mindedness. Although a significant part of his oeuvre was devoted to education and he had a long-lasting influence on radical and later socialist teachers, Multatuli is now hardly known as an educationist.[60] In a lecture addressed to an extraordinarily well-attended Sunday morning meeting of the organisation De Dageraad he spoke about what he called 'liberal education'.[61] His central thought was that the study of physics was by far preferable to religious education, but he also stressed the physical aspects of liberal education. Many

---

[56]Scheltema, 'Wat is beschaving', 8.

[57]See note 41.

[58]But note that even *De Gids* (the guide), the most important Dutch cultural journal of the nineteenth century, never had more than two thousand subscribers in that century, see Remieg Aerts, *De Letterheren: Liberale Cultuur in De Negentiende Eeuw: Het Tijdschrift De Gids* (Amsterdam: Meulenhoff, 1997), 15.

[59]'Notulenboek. 21.9.1862–18.6.1865' (minutes of the meetings of De Dageraad, February 8, 1863) 2.6.1. Archive Vrijdenkersvereniging 'De Dageraad', IISH.

[60]For Multatuli, freethinkers and education, see Piet Hoekman, 'Vrij van "spokery". Vrijdenkers over opvoeding en onderwijs', in *God noch autoriteit*, 192–217.

[61]Bokkel, *Gidsen en genieën*, 87–88. The lecture was published in part three of Multatuli's *Ideën*, published between 1869 and 1871. Here we are quoting from the edition published by F. Domela Nieuwenhuis: *Multatuli over vrije studie* (Amsterdam: Volksbibliotheek, 1913).

mothers, especially in the higher ranks of society, were more preoccupied with doing what was socially accepted than with what was good for children from a natural perspective. By dressing their infants in ridiculous clothes they clearly demonstrated that showing off their children to impress the neighbours was more important to them than raising them in accordance with natural principles. He especially denounced what he called obstructing the infant's body: hindering the young child from physically developing itself freely, just as older children were hindered from developing themselves intellectually. Multatuli was especially thinking of such practices as swaddling the infant or cradle-rocking, which according to him caused the infant's brain to turn into pulp. A better understanding of the physical needs of the child would prevent this. Multatuli's goal in education was, besides criticising middle-class educational practices, to create authentic people, free in their thinking and true to nature, an aim that according to him was often unfortunately thwarted in the early physical development of children.[62] Like Junghuhn and Scheltema, whom he honoured as great spirits, and many other freethinkers, Multatuli hinted that physical education should acquire the place it deserved in the overall development of the child.[63]

Conclusion

In this article, we have tried to show that physical education in the Netherlands in the mid-nineteenth century was understood in roughly two ways. One view we discussed was put forward by the philanthropic Society for Public Welfare and the leading writers in the field of physical education, Rijkens and Euler, who were driven by the idea of the social usefulness of gymnastics. They argued that a person could not function properly in society if his or her body was not well trained, which made it important for primary schools to offer physical education. A second and different position was taken by the freethinkers, a small and non-conformist group who challenged educational ideas with arguments derived from their naturalistic worldview, although they shared with Rijkens and Euler the conviction that the symbiotic relationship between body and mind was crucial to the proper understanding of education. Freethinkers, like Franz Junghuhn, S.P. Scheltema and Multatuli, took nature as their key concept and embraced the idea that stimulating the physical development of the child, in accordance with its physical needs and not hindered by cultural and social norms, contributed to the education of man towards human excellence or true humanity.

By opposing education for social usefulness, freethinkers were not aiming at the downfall of Dutch society. On the contrary, they interpreted the so-called progress of civilisation as perverting and false. According to freethinkers, forcing children to grow up unnaturally, disciplining them to act and live in a way that was unhealthy to themselves, was not in the interest of society. In their eyes, the harmonious and holistic education of the child, without paying attention to social and cultural norms, would create balanced and healthy human beings who would benefit society in the long run.

---

[62]*Multatuli over vrije studie*, 5–8.
[63]Multatuli mentioned Scheltema and Junghuhn in idea 482, see *Ideën van Multatuli*, part 2 (Amsterdam: R.C. Meijer, 1865).

How far the Dutch situation was unique to the Netherlands or rather reflected similar educational ideas in other Western nations has yet to be researched. By relating to Saure's study on physical educational thought in nineteenth-century Germany, we have shown that the ideas on physical education of the leading writers of the Romantic Movement in Germany closely corresponded to the pedagogic thought of the Dutch freethinkers. This does not yet prove the existence of a broader trend, but it does confirm that physical education could be seen as more than just 'the corporeal foundation of the modern state'.

Acknowledgements

The authors would like to thank Sjoerd Karsten, Bert Gasenbeek, Elise van Alphen and the anonymous reviewers for commenting on earlier versions of this article.

Exercise and education: facilities for the young female body in Scotland, 1930–1960

Eilidh H.R. Macrae

Sports Development, Abertay University, Dundee, Scotland, UK

This article uses testimony gathered from oral history interviews and contemporary physical education sources to explore the schooling of the young female body in Scotland between 1930 and 1960. It looks at the ways in which girls were educated about their own bodies and their physical capabilities at school, taking into account official understandings of the adolescent female body and how these may have affected girls' experiences of exercise. The article examines the ways through which girls negotiated the particularities of their adolescent female bodies throughout their exercise experiences, and specifically how they learned about and coped with menstruation and body changes. It argues that the school environment within which most Scottish girls would first have been exposed to exercise would hardly have been conducive to the formation of a healthy relationship between girls and their bodies.

Introduction

The history of British physical education (PE) is a subject in much need of further study, but in recent decades historians such as Jennifer Hargreaves, John Welshman, Kathleen McCrone and Charles Webster have made significant contributions to the topic.[1] Similarly, Sheila Fletcher's research has vastly improved our understanding of the origin and specifics of the 'female tradition' in English physical education.[2] Much like more contemporary sociological works such as Sheila Scraton's *Shaping up to Womanhood*, Fletcher demonstrates the merits of examining the PE lesson from a gendered perspective, and focuses upon the crucial role which female PE

---

[1] Jennifer Hargreaves, Sporting Females: Critical Issues in the History and Sociology of *Women's Sports* (London: Routledge, 1994); John Welshman, 'Physical Culture and Sport in Schools in England and Wales, 1900–1940', *International Journal of the History of Sport* 15, (1998): 54–75; Kathleen McCrone, *Playing the Game: Sport and the Physical Emancipation of English Women, 1870–1914* (Kentucky: University Press of Kentucky, 1988); Charles Webster, 'The Health of the School Child During the Depression', in *The Fitness of the Nation: Physical Education in the Nineteenth and Twentieth Centuries*, ed. N. Parry and D. McNair (Leicester: History of Education Society, 1983), 76–81.
[2] Sheila Fletcher, *Women First: The Female Tradition in English Physical Education 1880–1980* (London: Athlone Press, 1984).

teachers played in the birth and development of the subject.[3] David Kirk's numerous works have provided a post-war perspective which enhances our understanding of the history of British physical education, and in particular the gendered dimensions of the teaching culture within this sphere.[4] Kirk's research into Australian school sport also contributes to the growing body of work which looks at the history of physical education internationally, but our understanding of Scottish PE, and in particular pupil experiences, is still in its infancy.[5]

Recent studies by Fiona Skillen have improved this situation for the interwar period.[6] Skillen's work examines state intervention in girls' physical education and she highlights the presence of eugenicist, moral and social influences within the newly established Scottish PE curriculum of the 1930s.[7] Yet, we still have little understanding of how the post-war PE lesson was experienced by those adolescent Scottish girls who took part. Therefore this article will contribute an original perspective to this growing historiography of British PE history by using government, medical and oral history evidence to explore the schooling of the young female body in Scotland between 1930 and 1960. The article will argue that many Scottish schools lacked appropriate facilities that catered to the particular needs of adolescent girls taking part in PE lessons. By not recognising these adolescents as the physically mature young women they were and providing for them accordingly, officials presented these girls with what was often an uncomfortable and unattractive first contact with physical exercise.

By the 1930s most schoolgirls in Scotland had access to some form of physical activity and were being urged to appreciate the importance of exercise in day-to-day life. Throughout previous decades a system of physical education had gradually been established which, by this time, had come to incorporate various forms of team games, gymnastics and even swimming. This article will explore the experiences of eight women, born between 1921 and 1948, who came into contact with the Scottish system of physical education as adolescent girls and attempted to negotiate this school environment and curriculum whilst undergoing the often unforgiving physiological changes of adolescence. The school-day experiences of these women varied sharply in accordance with their social class or the locality within which they spent their adolescent years: they attended a wide variety of schools and were from both middle-class and working-class backgrounds, and as a result we can see that social class and locality certainly affected the way in which girls experienced the PE lesson, with regard to the variety of sports that were on offer to them at their particular school. Yet, despite their varied experiences in respect of

---

[3]Sheila Scraton, *Shaping up to Womanhood: Gender and Girls' Physical Education* (Buckingham: Open University Press, 1992).

[4]David Kirk, *Defining Physical Education: The Social Construction of a School Subject in Postwar Britain* (London: Falmer Press, 1992); David Kirk, 'Physical Education: A Gendered History', in *Gender and Physical Education: Contemporary Issues and Future Directions*, ed. D. Penney (London: Routledge, 2002), 24–37; David Kirk, *The Body, Schooling and Culture* (Victoria: Deakin University Press, 1993).

[5]David Kirk, 'Gender Associations: Sport, State Schools and Australian Culture', *International Journal of the History of Sport* 17, no. 2 (2000): 49–64.

[6]Fiona Skillen, '"A Sound System of Physical Training": The Development of Girls' Physical Education in Interwar Scotland', *History of Education*, 38, no. 3 (2009), 403–18; Fiona Skillen, '"When Women Look their Worst": Women and Sports Participation in Interwar Scotland' (PhD Thesis, University of Glasgow, 2008).

[7]Ibid.

the PE class itself and what was on offer to them, there was one element of adolescence that was common to all the interviewees: they had a lack of understanding of their own female bodies and were often unprepared for the physiological changes they encountered during puberty. With a lack of appreciation on the part of officials with regard to providing information and facilities to aid the physiological transition of adolescence, and a prevailing taboo of discussion of such issues in the home, many of these girls had to manage their body changes secretly, and often with great distress and confusion. Whilst the official PE curriculum continued to be developed throughout the mid-twentieth century, the experiences of girls on the ground was at odds with the official picture of an established and varied physical education curriculum which attended to the needs of boys and girls alike.

Development of physical education in Scotland

A girl's experience of physical exercise within the 1930s Scottish school could vary sharply throughout the country, mostly in accordance with the type of school and whether it had the funds to provide equipment for a varied PE lesson. In 1930 Miss A.N. Kyle, of the Dunfermline Physical Training College '1928 set' of graduating teachers, and a recently appointed PE teacher at Renfrew High School, stressed that she still enjoyed teaching there although 'the promised Gymnasium [had] not materialised so far'.[8] Similarly, in 1932 Miss I. Dickson of the '1929 set' appealed to her fellow PE graduates in the Old Students' Association Magazine for anyone who had 'an old [pommel gymnastics] horse to spare? However dilapidated? They are very scarce up here', this being in her teaching post at Inverurie in Aberdeenshire where gym equipment was apparently in poor supply.[9] In the same year Miss I.R. Carmichael was employed in six schools in Renfrewshire based in Greenock, Gourock and Port Glasgow, noting that although the work was very interesting it was 'nearly all outdoor', suggesting that of these six schools few had indoor gym facilities.[10] This evidence of poor gym equipment or even a complete lack of indoor gym facilities in some schools is notable when we consider David Kirk's suggestion that, 'from the 1880s up to the 1950s, gymnastics was the main content of physical education programmes in government schools'.[11] If facilities in some Scottish schools were so poor that a Swedish gymnastics class performed in an equipped gymnasium was an impossibility, and the Scottish weather was less than favourable to outdoor work, as would often have been a reality throughout the school year, it is doubtful as to whether girls could have had a wholly positive and varied experience of physical exercise throughout their school lives.

Nevertheless, as Skillen has argued, prior to the 1930s the government had been aiming to enhance the position of physical education within the school-life of the child, with their efforts being realised in the new Scottish curriculum introduced in 1931.[12] The importance of the physical training of the young body had been

---

[8] Edinburgh University Special Collections (EUSC) (currently not catalogued) *Dunfermline College of Hygiene 1914–1936, Old Students Association, Dunfermline Physical Training College, 18th Annual Report: 1929–1930*, 26.

[9] EUSC *Dunfermline College of Hygiene 1914–1936, Old Students Association, Dunfermline Physical Training College, 20th Annual Report: 1931–32*, 19.

[10] Ibid., 16.

[11] Kirk, 'Physical Education: A Gendered History', 25.

[12] Skillen, 'When Women Look their Worst', 17.

prominent in the minds of some educators for decades. From 1885, and the opening of Martina Bergmann-Osterberg's pioneering training college for women in London, the prominent female role and interest in this sphere was established, with the Scottish equivalent opening as the Women's College of Hygiene and Physical Training at Dunfermline in 1905.[13] In the years prior to the establishment of Dunfermline College, prospective Scottish PE teachers had to travel to the English colleges for their training.[14] Encouraged by the findings of the *Report of the Royal Commission on Physical Training in Scotland*, published in 1903, the Dunfermline Trust sought to contribute to the efforts being made throughout the country to improve the deteriorating health of children in Scotland.[15] It was assumed by the men who formed the committee of Carnegie's Dunfermline Trust that the opening of a PE college in Dunfermline would not only enhance the physical health of Scotland's children by increasing the local pool of available teachers, but it would also bring prestige and benefit to the community of Dunfermline.[16] As a result of these links to Carnegie, the women's PE College at Dunfermline quickly developed a prominent reputation as an elite institution.

This 'female tradition' of physical education, where female physical educators dominated this teaching sphere, helped to create the illusion that girls' physical education was suitably advanced and that girls' physical health was well catered for, perhaps even more so than that of the boys.[17] Yet the form of physical education that girls were exposed to in the early twentieth century was limited and based on strict principles which perhaps did well to promote a certain restricted and controlled type of female physicality, but did little to excite and encourage girls to seek out their physical potentials.[18] The Swedish gymnastics of Per Henrik Ling formed the basis of much of the PE class, where precise free-standing movements were performed on command in a style not unlike military drill.[19] The gymnastics tradition was quite specifically female at this time in that very few male teachers took an interest or played a part in the spread of this form of exercise through British schools. Rather there was a simultaneous, but quite detached, trend in male physical education whereby boys were trained in the 'upper class games ethic' through the playing of games such as rugby football.[20] Since the late nineteenth century Scottish educators had made attempts to instil in middle-class boys that illustrious quality of good British 'character' through the moralising process of playing team

---

[13]S. Fletcher, 'The Making and Breaking of a Female Tradition: Women's Physical Education in England 1880–1980', in *From 'Fair Sex' to Feminism: Sport and the Socialization of Women in the Industrial and Post-Industrial Era*, ed. J.A. Mangan and R.J. Park (London: Frank Cass, 1987), 148.

[14]One such example was Flora Ogston, an upper-middle-class woman from Aberdeen, who attended Chelsea College of Physical Education from 1901 to 1903 but returned to Scotland to teach; I.C. MacLean, *The History of Dunfermline College of Physical Education* (1976), 34.

[15]National Archives of Scotland (NAS), ED71/23, *Report of the Royal Commission on Physical Training in Scotland* (Edinburgh: HMSO, 1903), 27–8.

[16]MacLean, *The History of Dunfermline College of Physical Education*, 34.

[17]Fletcher, 'The Making and Breaking of a Female Tradition', 148.

[18]Scraton, *Shaping up to Womanhood*, 13.

[19]Fletcher, 'The Making and Breaking of a Female Tradition', 147, 152.

[20]D. Kirk, 'Curriculum History in Physical Education: A Source of Struggle and a Force for Change', in *Research in Physical Education and Sport: Exploring Alternative Visions*, ed. A. C. Sparkes (London: Falmer Press, 1992), 221.

games, and so these forms of school exercise had a strong historical attachment to these particular schools.[21] However, whilst games had been gradually assimilated into the curriculum for Scottish boys by the early twentieth century, games and girls were not deemed to be quite so compatible. Most games were employed to encourage competitiveness, physical strength and confidence, and these were the prime values which the teachers in the upper- and middle-class boys' schools hoped would be ingrained in their pupils. Yet, these were characteristics that did not sit well within the educators' views of the ideal schoolgirl, particularly when these schoolgirls were eventually to become mothers and wives.

In the first few decades of the twentieth century women were viewed primarily as the mothers or future mothers of the race and the separate spheres discourse prevailed.[22] The far-reaching power of this discursive construction had repercussions in all areas of female life and it most certainly had an effect on the type of contact that could occur between young girls and sport. Mangan and Loughlan have suggested that competitive sport, within the context of the boys' school and when combined with good mental schooling, was viewed as a healthy way to ensure that Scottish boys had a good grounding in the mentality of confidence that was popular with their English counterparts, and it was assumed this would set them up well for employment south of the Border.[23] But there was little social requirement for schoolgirls to take on games in the same manner, it being assumed that after school, even if they did take up a working life periodically, they would ultimately be restricted to the domestic sphere once they embarked upon marriage and motherhood. The enhancement of employability through the encouragement of a competitive nature and personal confidence were not characteristics that were assumed to be required of the Scottish wife and mother of the early twentieth century.

Despite this, some leading girls' schools significantly increased the variety of activities that could be 'acceptably' introduced into the girls' curriculum during these early years. As Fletcher has shown, a solid collection of girls' public schools had been established in Britain by the late nineteenth century.[24] Much like the new women's colleges which were opened in the 1870s at Cambridge and Oxford, the English institutions of female learning were shaped by middle-class ideals of quality and respectability within which the contemporary form of girls' physical education could thrive, and St Leonard's School in St Andrews was no different.[25] St Leonard's was a private school for girls founded in 1877 and, in keeping with the style of PE in similar English schools, the pupils here were introduced to a wide variety of games such as hockey, lacrosse, cricket and tennis.[26] Private girls' schools like

---

[21]J.A. Mangan and C. Loughlan, 'Fashion and Fealty: The Glaswegian Bourgeoisie, Middle-Class Schools and the Games-Ethic in the Victorian and Edwardian Eras', *International Journal of the History of Sport* 5, no. 1 (1988): 133–5.

[22]For discussion of the 'separate spheres' discourse see L. Davidoff and C. Hall, *Family Fortunes: Men and Women of the English Middle Class, 1780 – 1850* (London: Hutchinson, 1987); E. Gordon and G. Nair, *Public Lives: Women, Family and Society in Victorian Britain* (London: Yale University Press, 2003); M. Vicinus, ed., *Suffer and Be Still: Women in the Victorian Age* (London: Indiana University Press, 1973).

[23]Mangan and Loughlan, 'Fashion and Fealty', 135.

[24]Fletcher, *Women First*, 16.

[25]Ibid.

[26]*St Leonard's School Magazine, 1920–1938* (St Leonards School Archive), in Skillen, 'When Women Look their Worst', 32.

St Leonard's had the means to provide their pupils with this wide variety of games and activities, but this varied PE programme was largely only a reality for the few wealthy or well-positioned rural schools where space and funds were in no short supply. Yet, there was a particular team game on offer during these years which could be easily played in urban state schools as it required little equipment and was deemed to be particularly 'suited' to girls: this game was netball.

The emergence of netball as the quintessential female competitive game is a phenomenon that Mandy Treagus has explored in some detail. Despite the assumption that games were unnecessary for girls as far as promoting cultural life-skills was concerned, rather Treagus suggests that games such as netball did indeed prepare girls for their life-roles as mothers and wives, and this is supposedly what made it so suitable. Treagus argues that, through this game, girls were coached in the act of bodily restraint and personal sacrifice for the sake of the team, skills which would be useful when carrying out their roles as reserved mothers who put their family's interests before their own.[27] The personal glory and physical confidence which would be instilled in boys through games like rugby, where the physical tackling of other boys was actively encouraged, were alien concepts within the ethos of netball. In this game, girls had to learn to restrain their bodies by not travelling when they held the ball and by avoiding physical contact with other players, retaining their own personal space and not impinging on that of others. In any case, netball appeared to be a popular game with teachers and pupils alike. Being a relatively cheap game requiring few pieces of apparatus and being playable both indoors and out, it could be enjoyed by girls in those schools where activities such as hockey games played on proper pitches were an unattainable dream. The experiences of girls growing up in Scotland in the 1930s, 1940s and even 1950s were varied and seldom strictly reflected the recommendations of educationists or even the official curriculum, but all the interviewees in this study recalled playing netball at school and so it appears to have been a widely accessible sport.

The women who were interviewed for this study attended a range of schools in the Glasgow area, Aberdeenshire, West Lothian and Ayrshire, and it is evident that those who happened to be from a locality where the main school was not particularly modern had significantly different experiences from those who attended fee-paying or newly built schools. Of the eight interviewees, Betty, Margaret H. and Christine grew up in working-class households in the Glasgow area and they attended local schools, though Margaret received a scholarship and attended the fee-paying Hutchesons' Grammar School. Helen grew up in West Lothian and Mary grew up in Stevenston in Ayrshire: both were brought up in working-class families and attended their local state schools. Anne grew up in Aberdeenshire, Linda in Uddingston near Glasgow, and Margaret B. in Yorkshire although she moved to Stirling in later life. These last three women had middle-class backgrounds but still attended their local state schools. None of the interviewees were Catholic and so they all attended the non-denominational state schools on offer in their locality, and it is therefore these types of Scottish schools which the following discussion will focus upon. Their adolescent PE experiences would have been within all-female pupil environments as boys and girls were timetabled separately

---

[27]M. Treagus, 'Playing like Ladies: Basketball, Netball and Feminine Restraint', *International Journal of the History of Sport* 22, no. 1 (2005): 90.

for PE after they reached secondary school.[28] This separation was a clear acknowledgement of the imminent physiological changes which would supposedly alter the ways in which boys and girls experienced exercise, and alter the effect that certain types of exercise, such as competitive games, would have on their bodies and character.[29]

Throughout the interviews it quickly became clear that a girl's social class did not necessarily play a fundamental role in shaping her exercise experiences. Rather, how modern her local school building was, and whether her childhood was spent in an urban or rural locality, were both more significant. For example, Anne grew up in Aberdeenshire in the 1940s in a middle-class family and developed a great love of sport through her participation outside school, later going on to become a physical education teacher, but we can see from the following interview excerpt that the facilities in her own school were quite poor:

Q: ...What were the facilities like, you played hockey and things, did you have your own pitch...?

A: No (laugh), the school was ancient. Eh, we, we had a field which really belonged to the big estate. We played in front of the big house which was unoccupied.

...

Q: Was there any, where did you get changed or did you just come –

A: Under the tree (laugh). Uhuh, behind the bushes.

Q: ... just at the side, yeah.

A: There were no changing rooms, no.[30]

Despite coming from a relatively affluent family, with her father owning a successful shoe shop, Anne's local school was still relatively poorly equipped for sport, and this affected her PE experiences. Of course, those girls whose families were affluent enough to allow them to attend any of the well-equipped private girls' schools would clearly have had more varied PE lessons, but the majority of participants in these interviews were from lower middle-class or working-class families where the regional distinction was more applicable. Even so, these regional distinctions could be striking: other interviewees recalled the existence of changing rooms, and some even had their own swimming pools and showers, such as Bellahouston Academy in Glasgow, so certainly Anne's school experience was not standard. But what does appear to have been standard throughout this time was the general understandings of the physical capabilities of girls' bodies, and lack of knowledge or appreciation of their inner workings, by both the girls themselves and officials who had the power to structure their experiences at school. Moreover, the continuity of

---

[28]NAS, ED8/15, *Report of the Third Advisory Council on Education in Scotland: Sub-Committee on Physical Education and Character Training in Schools* (1932), 2.
[29]Ibid.
[30]'Anne', interview by the author, October 28, 2010 (all interviews were conducted in confidentiality and so pseudonyms have been used throughout).

this lack of knowledge and appreciation of the particularities of the young female body from the mid-1930s through to the 1950s, and perhaps even beyond, is quite striking. Yet, we can see that from the early twentieth century education officials had been developing the way in which schoolchildren came into contact with sport and exercise at school. They certainly acknowledged the physiological differences between the sexes in their production of the curriculum, albeit perhaps not in a way that would have helped girls to manage their adolescent bodies whilst they participated in this curriculum.

'The young and growing organism': physical and health education 1930–1960

By the early 1930s the health of the Scottish child had been a concern of the Scottish Education Department (SED) for some time and since 1908 the new School Medical Service had been playing its part in aiding the situation through inspection and treatment of the schoolchild.[31] The School Medical Service had been established by the Education (Scotland) Act of 1908 after the findings of a 1903 Royal Commission into the health of schoolchildren in Scotland had uncovered an unsettling degree of physical ill health amongst the urban populations.[32] The causes of the health problems were thought to be, amongst others, overcrowding, lack of fresh air, poor diet and insufficient official inspection of public places such as schools and workplaces.[33] Through the new medical inspections, a physical education programme and the distribution of free meals and milk at school, in the first three decades of the twentieth century the SED attempted to both cure the already unhealthy schoolchild and prevent the supposedly inevitable deterioration of the healthy child.[34]

Nevertheless, from their introduction in 1908 the realistic improvements that could be reaped from the inspections themselves were limited. The inspections were brief and ideally designed to outline serious physical problems such as deafness or physical disability but many health problems would have gone undetected. Indeed, statistics published in 1929 appear to support this lack of detection. The Annual Report of the Department of Health for Scotland showed that from the school medical examinations of 1929, within which 33.3% of all Scottish children were inspected, supposedly only 6.1% of these children showed signs of poor nutrition, 0.1% had obvious signs of tuberculosis, only 1.8% had head lice, 5.8% had poor eyesight and 3.7% had any skin diseases.[35] However, it has been suggested that this sample was far from representative. In reference to these statistics, the medical doctor and historian Morrice McCrae has noted that 'based on my own many years' experience of Scottish children, I find these figures almost incredible. I would have found them surprisingly good even 30 years later.'[36] It would appear that the

---

[31]M. McCrae, *The National Health Service in Scotland: Origins and Ideals, 1900–1950* (East Lothian: Tuckwell Press, 2003), 6.

[32]*Report of the Royal Commission on Physical Training (Scotland)* (1903), Cd. 1507, in McCrae, *The National Health Service in Scotland*, 12.

[33]*Report of the Inter Departmental Committee on Physical Deterioration*, 1904, Cd. 2175, in McCrae, *The National Health Service in Scotland*, 13.

[34]Skillen, 'When Women Look their Worst', 21–2.

[35]'School Medical Examinations, Scotland, 1929', *Annual Report of the Department of Health for Scotland, 1929*, in McCrae, *The National Health Service in Scotland*, 13.

[36]McCrae, *The National Health Service in Scotland*, 142.

detection of physical defects in the Scottish child was not assured by the school medical inspection.

Moreover, even when physical defects were identified in a child, treatment of the defect was not necessarily forthcoming. Before 1918 medical inspectors could advise parents to seek medical treatment for their child but the parents may not have had the funds, or indeed the trust in the opinion of the medical expert, to follow it up. This changed in 1918 when local education authorities were advised to provide limited forms of treatment for the children when necessary, such as provision of spectacles and hospital treatment for those with tuberculosis or heart disease.[37] Yet even in the early 1930s the poor health of the British schoolchild was still viewed as a great concern within the medical community. A 1932 article in the *Lancet* based on a speech delivered to an audience at the Royal College of Physicians of London by Dr L.P. Jacks, the principal of Oxford's Manchester College, showed something of the concerns of contemporary medics regarding young children: 'a large proportion of these human bodies show unmistakable signs of being *damaged*, not in the sense of being mutilated, but in the sense of being defective, devitalised, and inadequate'.[38] The economic depression of the 1930s, and unprecedented unemployment figures of almost three million people out of work by 1932, certainly contributed to the rapid deterioration of the health of many British children during this period.[39] Throughout the 1930s officials acquired a stream of evidence which showed a stark prevalence of diseases of malnutrition amongst children from the poorer social classes, and particularly amongst those families affected by unemployment.[40] In 1934 the government made an attempt to combat this through the introduction of free school meals and milk for the most impoverished children.[41] Yet it would appear that, despite these developments, officials were not prepared to provide substantial public funds to improve the state of facilities and supply of sports equipment in state schools at this time. Moreover, it was noted by certain officials that nutrition should be the primary focus over and above any interference in sport and the physical education system, as it was dangerous to encourage a malnourished individual to exercise.[42] As the 1930s progressed, there appeared to be a growing enthusiasm amongst officials for improving physical fitness amongst Britons as demonstrated by the national fitness campaign of 1937, which aimed to enhance the fitness of all people in Britain, though mostly those above school age, and yet there were various factors that delayed any substantial development of public sports facilities at this time.[43] The onset of the Second World War in 1939, followed by extended rationing into the post-war years, and the Labour government's prioritisation of economic recovery and national security over investment and development of sports facilities, meant that it would be the mid-1960s before any significant public money was directed towards the improvement

---

[37]Ibid., 143.

[38]L.P. Jacks, 'The Liberal Education of the Body', *Lancet*, November 26, 1932, 1146.

[39]J. Stevenson and C. Cook, *The Slump: Britain in the Great Depression* (London: Longman, 2010), 53.

[40]Ibid.

[41]Stevenson and Cook, *The Slump: Britain in the Great Depression*, 53.

[42]'Bases of National Fitness', *Lancet*, November 21, 1936, 1219.

[43]For a full discussion of the national fitness campaign in Scotland see E. Macrae, '"Scotland for Fitness": The National Fitness Campaign and Scottish Women', *Women's History Magazine* (Spring, 2010): 26–36.

of school and public sports facilities.[44] Therefore, as a result of huge regional variations in terms of access to funds and space within which to make improvements to facilities, the overall picture of Scottish PE remained largely unchanged between the interwar and post-war years.

As has been noted above, the facilities available to schools varied widely across Britain. Skillen has shown that in the interwar period there were great gaps between what the syllabus advocated for the ideal PE lesson and what was possible given the poor level of financial support available to fund any advances.[45] There were also a variety of styles of physical exercise that could be called upon in the lesson, but although some officials strongly believed that children's bodies were degenerating in their urban environments and that something should be done to rectify this situation, they also believed that only certain carefully devised physical programmes were appropriate. In 1930 the school medical inspectors were still convinced of the importance of remedial gymnastics and massage as administered by the medical officers and PE instructors in schools, and there was a prevalent belief that through these measures they could 'cure' the health problems of schoolchildren. For example it was decided that the programme for a 1930 conference attended by education authorities and experts in PE 'should deal with ... Remedial Gymnastics mainly', with four days of classes on 'remedial gymnastics and massage' for 'school medical officers and physical instructors (men and women)'.[46] At this time officials appeared to be retaining their focus on corrective gymnastics and massage with an aim to cure the defective young bodies of Scotland. Yet the curriculum that was to be introduced the following year suggested a step in a different direction.

The 1931 curriculum aimed to tailor the PE class to enhance the 'moral and social training' of the child.[47] With this in mind, team games such as hockey, football and basketball or netball were encouraged to satisfy the 'self-testing, competitive, and cooperative impulse of pubescent and adolescent years' from within the controlled PE environment, presumably so that children did not seek to inappropriately satisfy these impulses in other areas of their social life outside the school.[48] Moreover, although all children were to be encouraged to take part in the team games, it was still stressed that 'on physiological grounds, the elements of keen competition in the case of girls require careful control'.[49] Within this document, no exact reasoning was given to explain the physiological science behind the dangers of competition for girls. However, the reference to the element of 'control' required by girls who took part in those competitive sports deemed suitable for their constitution, such as netball, harks back to the belief prevalent for centuries that women, as emotional creatures, were unsuited to the competitive public sphere.[50] But to note the importance of this control to be based on 'physiological' grounds suggested to contemporaries that this guideline was formed from the factual

---

[44]R. Holt and T. Mason, *Sport in Britain 1945–2000* (Oxford: Blackwell, 2000), 146.

[45]Skillen, 'When Women Look their Worst', 19.

[46]NAS GD1/1022/3, Association of School Medical Officers of Scotland, 'Minutes of Meeting 27th April 1929'.

[47]NAS CRE 3/1/3 Publications of the Scottish Council for Research in Education, *Curriculum for Pupils of Twelve to Fifteen Years, 1931, Reprint no 8: Physical Education*, 4.

[48]Ibid.

[49]Ibid.

[50]M. Jordanova, *Sexual Visions: Images of Gender in Science and Medicine between the Eighteenth and Twentieth Centuries* (London: Harvester Wheatsheaf, 1989), 23.

findings of medical experts, and thus should not be questioned. The idea that violent competitive sport was incompatible with the female form was still ingrained in the contemporary discursive framework, and this idea had its roots in the medical discourses of the recent past.[51] Although around the 1930s the attitudes of some doctors towards women and sport were changing, they still had a long way to go before general medical circles and the wider public accepted that vigorous exercise could be beneficial to girls' bodies. The adolescent body, and the physical capabilities of girls who were going through the changes of puberty, were topics that were to be debated within medical circles for years to come. Certain medical studies from as late as 1947 maintained arguments which stressed that the physiological changes of puberty had an adverse effect upon the athletic performance of girls, and that their PE lessons should be structured with this in mind: 'so far as running ability is concerned, puberty has an adverse effect.... Girls' performances over the 50-yard dash worsened between the ages of 13 and 16.'[52] Evidently, with this subject still a topic of debate amongst medical researchers, the restraining features of this gendered 1931 curriculum would probably have gone unquestioned in the majority of state schools. The SED was now reasonably open to the idea that girls should also be given the chance to play 'suitable' team games, but when viewed from within the discursive framework this could only be possible if certain gendered guidelines were upheld and, most importantly, if the female body was not damaged in the process.

Despite various advances in the medical community's view of the compatibility of women and sport, in the 1930s women were primarily viewed as the mothers or future mothers of the race and if vigorous exercise was thought to damage this fundamental female function it could not be condoned.[53] Throughout these years many debates centred upon the potential damage that sport could do to the female body, and from the 1931 curriculum it would appear that both the male and female adolescent years were viewed as distinctive developmental stages which had to be carefully considered in reference to physical education:

> A consideration of the physiological and psychological changes that take place within the organism during the outset of pubescence and adolescence, as well as the widening differences between boys and girls in these respects, should be primary factors impressing a distinctive character on the training of each of the sexes. The physical education of boys and girls of post-qualifying classes should accordingly be in the hands of specialist teachers of physical training – men and women respectively.[54]

Whilst the early physical education of the child in elementary school was practically identical for boys and girls up until the age of 12, officials identified some necessity for a clear distinction of the sexes to be made at the onset of puberty.[55] This must

---

[51]See for example 'President's address, delivered at The Fifty-fourth Annual meeting of the British Medical Association, Held in Brighton, August 10th–13th, 1886', *British Medical Journal* 2 (August 14, 1886): 296.

[52]'Education of the Body', *Lancet*, July 26, 1947, 139.

[53]See for example 'President's address, delivered at The Fifty-fourth Annual meeting of the British Medical Association'; 'Treatment of Cases of Abortion', *Lancet*, September 20, 1930, 654; 'Menstruation and Athletics', *Lancet*, February 13, 1932, 357–8.

[54]*Curriculum for Pupils of Twelve to Fifteen Years, 1931*, 6.

[55]NAS ED/8/15 Advisory Council, *Education Authority of Glasgow: Syllabus of Physical Training for Elementary Schools 1920*.

have had an effect upon the way in which girls viewed their involvement in exercise from this point forward. It is evident from the curriculum's earlier reference to the particular 'physiological' makeup of the young female body, which required careful care and 'control' throughout games, that the distinction lay in the vigorous and competitive nature in which it was possible for some games to be played. Girls were not to be encouraged to be competitive in the same way as boys, and for some girls there must have been a certain fear of the physical damage that they could inflict upon themselves if they increased their speed, played for longer than advised, or let their competitive spirit run wild. But what seemed to be clear throughout the interviews was that it was not the dangers of competition that young Scottish girls were worried about, rather, they worried about their bodies more generally and how they would practically manage their menstruating bodies whilst at school. Despite considering girls' bodies to be physiologically different, this was one very real aspect of the young female body which the officials seemed to have overlooked.

Knowledge of the body

Helen, an upper-working-class interviewee who grew up in the village of Uphall in West Lothian in the early 1940s, noted that she enjoyed the games which were on offer in her school but she was not so fond of the militaristic gymnastics classes:

A: But I enjoyed the netball and I enjoyed the hockey, yeah. I enjoyed all the things I took part in.

Q: What about the gymnastics type things and the, and the wall-bars was that, did that appeal to you?

A: Well, it didn't, but not as much as against it, ye know. I preferred the games, take part in the games, rather than going up the wall bars or the ropes, but I managed to do it and twist round and go up the wall-bars and things. But eh, I just did it 'cause we did it as a class but, eh, I preferred the games and liked to take part in games.[56]

Helen made it clear that it was not that she was incapable of doing the gymnastics, rather it just did not appeal to her, but she enjoyed the more interesting aspects of games such as netball and hockey. It was during Helen's discussion of her enjoyment of games that she naturally brought her narrative round to the particular way in which she experienced games as a young woman with a developing body. Despite being very physically active at this time of life, and throughout her later life where she continued a variety of activities, Helen noted that on reflection she was quite ignorant about the functions of her own body generally whilst growing up. This was a prevalent theme throughout many of the interviews and there seemed to be a sense that the reality of the inner workings of the female body, puberty and reproduction were things which could still not be openly discussed whilst these women were experiencing adolescence. Helen noted a lack of health education in the school and at home, and this is shown through her telling of the shock when she first started her period and was clueless about the entire process:

---

[56]'Helen', interview by the author, May 18, 2010.

A: Aye, well I was just active. I mean, I suppose nowadays they know more about things than we did. Because, at thirteen when I got my periods I didn't know what they were, ye know? My mother had to explain it. And it's just, twelve, thirteen when I got it, I wondered just...

Q: So did your mum chat to you about that?

A: Uhuh, and when I got it I said, 'I've hurt myself', and she says 'No, you haven't.' She, I recall that. That I said, 'I've hurt myself', and she says, 'No, you haven't'.

Q: And she explained, yeah.

A: And I wasn't aware of. Hadn't talked to other girls about it. I mean, nowadays I know it would be different. In those days I got it and I didn't know what it was. And she explained it.[57]

There is a clear feeling in Helen's testimony that times have now changed for the better in terms of girls' knowledge of the physical workings of their bodies. She makes a distinction between then and now, and implicitly praises the subsequent introduction of detailed health education in schools, outlining the era of her child-hood as a time of ignorance for girls. Indeed throughout the 1940s and even on into the 1960s and beyond there was discussion about the benefits and dangers of the introduction of sex and health education in schools, but little progress was actually made in this area and an official curriculum was not established during these early years. Despite this, there were certain campaigners within the official sphere who attempted to convince the Educational Institute of Scotland (EIS), the teachers' union, of the benefits of the inclusion of this form of education. In 1943 the Scottish Council for Health Education was set up 'to promote and encourage educa-tion in healthy living'.[58] Within this remit, it aimed to enhance health education of young people and a Continuing Committee was established to research and devise a suitable scheme for schools. Yet, despite uncovering some findings which certainly supported the introduction of a detailed health education curriculum, still the EIS failed to use its power to alter the situation.[59]

A speech made by Tom Fraser, the Under-Secretary of State for Scotland, in 1949, clearly stressed that the contemporary code for day schools noted that health education was to be taught in an 'appropriate form throughout the child's school life'.[60] Nevertheless, it was not clear which subject teacher or department was responsible for dispensing these integral life-lessons, and with the lack of a national syllabus it was at the discrepancy of each individual head teacher as to what information should be provided. Research by the Continuing Committee in the late 1940s had led to the conclusion that:

> The head teacher is a key person in the health education programme in schools. His direct interest, or lack of it, determines success or failure. His enthusiasm stimulates

---

[57]Ibid.

[58]NAS ED/48/178 Health Education Curriculum, 'Speech Written for Mr Tom Fraser the Under-Secretary of State, 14/4/49', 2.

[59]NAS ED/48/178 Health Education Curriculum, *Report of the Scottish Council for Health Education, Scheme of Health Education for Schools. 15/7/50.*

[60]'Speech written for Mr Tom Fraser the Under-Secretary of State, 14/4/49', 2.

that of his teachers and without it their efforts may lack purposefulness and perhaps also lag.[61]

Consequently, the health education lessons that were given to girls throughout Scotland could vary widely in relation to what the views of their head teacher were regarding the necessity of instruction in this area.

In an attempt to improve the situation, experimental sex education courses were piloted with girls in two Edinburgh schools in 1947 and 1948. Norton Park Secondary School carried out a series of 40-minute weekly lessons with girls between 12 and 15 years of age during the summer term of 1947, and these were administered by Anabelle Duncan, a qualified midwife and experienced teacher. Duncan was also a member of the Alliance of Honour, a purity organisation established in London in 1903, and it was under the auspices of this group that she carried out these lessons. The interest of the Alliance of Honour in the health education of Scottish children was grounded in their aim to ensure children received the 'correct' information on sex and the body.[62] They tried to help youths to appreciate the importance of a wholesome family environment, and to ensure they understood the real responsibilities and consequences which might be attached to physical actions, so that they would have enough knowledge to resist their temptations to investigate and act upon their curiosities.

The second scheme was with 15- to 18-year-old girls at Leith Academy in 1948, and in both of these pilot schemes parents were initially contacted and invited to a group meeting where they could raise any concerns or grant their approval before the lessons took place, and indeed before they began 'it was manifest that the scheme had the unanimous approval of the mothers'.[63] This approval was obviously crucial, as a main reason behind exclusion of sex education from the curriculum in the past had been the belief that parents would wholly disapprove. Certainly the unanimous approval of the mothers who were involved in this scheme would suggest that official assumptions and beliefs concerning what parents ought to think with regard to their children gaining knowledge of sex in their early teenage years were quite detached from the reality of the situation, and the mothers here were keen for their daughters to be better informed.

Throughout the three weeks of lessons the biological workings of the body, reproduction, health, hygiene and the 'growing up' process were explained to the girls, although crucially there was 'particular reference to the family as the keystone of society' so that the educators could not be accused of encouraging promiscuity but rather of supplying facts to steer girls towards what they considered to be the right life-choices.[64] Interestingly, in the final week girls were invited to put forward anonymously hand-written questions, and 236 questions were received, suggesting a considerable level of confusion or ignorance. As the reported findings of the pilot scheme noted, 'the questions immediately revealed that the girls were already primed in many of the facts by their mothers, but that the information was often

---

[61]NAS ED/48/178, Health Education Curriculum, *The Scottish Council for Health Education: Report of the Committee on Health Education in Schools* (Edinburgh, 1950), 22–3.
[62]Roger Davidson and Gayle Davis, '"This Thorniest of Problems": School Sex Education Policy in Scotland 1939–80', *Scottish Historical Review* 84, no. 2 (October, 2005): 221–46.
[63]*Scottish Council for Health Education: Report of the Committee on Health Education in Schools*, 23–4.
[64]Ibid., 24.

misleading, if not false'.[65] Therefore, this underlined the essential need for health education within an official environment where rumours and doubt could be laid to rest upon the acquisition of the facts, and where it could be ensured all girls would receive this crucial information, which might not be supplied to them in the home. As shown by the experience of Helen, it could not always be ensured that the information would reach girls in time, and it would surely have been troubling and traumatic for a girl to experience but not understand her first period. For many girls growing up in the 1940s a lack of knowledge of the workings of their own bodies would have been a reality.

Understandably, when girls were told by their elders, peers, or by officials or 'experts' in society that vigorous physical exercise could damage the female body, they did not have the appropriate factual knowledge about the strength or physical workings of their own bodies to think anything else. The EIS was presented with the findings of the Continuing Committee's investigations but despite what appeared to be overwhelming evidence showing that health education was badly needed within Scottish schools, the Educational Institute maintained its previous stance, which was against inclusion. A representative of the EIS, Mr Allardice, explained in correspondence with the Committee that the EIS 'wanted to avoid ... the imposing of the scheme on the teachers of Scotland before they were ready for it and before a proper means of carrying it into effect had been thought out', suggesting that they were unconvinced by the efforts of the Committee in the pilot scheme.[66] Yet the Continuing Committee were eager to stress that it was crucial that the scheme was not wholly discarded but indeed simply better 'thought out' before it was fully introduced. Mr Frizell, of the Continuing Committee, noted his belief that 'instruction in personal relations or sex education was long overdue ... there had been real cowardice on the part of all concerned ... generations of young people had gone into the world ill-prepared and with distorted views of one of the most vital matters of life', and in this it would seem he was quite accurate. Nevertheless, sex education programmes continued to be administered on an 'ad hoc' basis well into the 1970s and beyond, with much variation in content and detail of instruction throughout the country.[67] Thus, the era of doubt and ignorance experienced by Helen in her schooldays of the 1940s continued and affected the experiences of girls for years to come.

A lack of facilities for the young female body

Whilst there was a failure to supply an adequate level of instruction in health and hygiene to girls growing up in 1940s Scotland, it would also appear that girls were seldom catered for in terms of the provision of facilities which would help them to keep clean and healthy whilst at school. The speech given by Tom Fraser at an April 1949 conference attended by officials interested in the health education profession commented on the poor facilities of the contemporary Scottish schools: 'insufficient wash-basins, inadequate latrines, too few clean towels – prevent the

---

[65]Ibid., 24.

[66]NAS ED/48/178, Health Education Curriculum, 'Report of the Scottish Council for Health Education, Scheme of Health Education for Schools. Report of Meeting with EIS Representatives, 15/7/50'.

[67]Davidson and Davis, '"This Thorniest of Problems"', 244.

schools setting the high example which plays such an effective part in education'.[68] Mary, a working-class interviewee who went to school in Stevenston in Ayrshire in the late 1940s, recalled the poor facilities at her school where the washing amenities themselves were unclean and unattractive, and she felt she was not catered for appropriately 'as a female':

Q: What about changing rooms and?

A: These were minimal, ye know. They weren't, they weren't really, there was limited showers and they weren't very good or nice or clean or anything like that so I would say that the standards of the changing rooms were very poor.

Q: What about things, mirrors or anything like that, washing?

A: No, that wasn't, you were never catered for as a female, a young female ye know. And eh, it was bare.[69]

Mary's indication that she was not catered for as a 'young female' points to her belief that there was a lack of understanding by officials of the growing-up process for girls and the ways this process could have been made easier and less traumatic.

Certainly, a key element of personal hygiene for young girls at school, given that many girls were now staying on at school beyond the early teenage years, was keeping clean and comfortable throughout menstruation. Yet, a study carried out by the Menstrual Hygiene Subcommittee of the Medical Women's Federation and reported in the *Lancet* in May 1949 showed that the situation in schools throughout Britain was far from adequate.[70] In an attempt to collect information about the methods available for the acquisition of sanitary towels and for changing and disposing of them within school, the Subcommittee had approached Dr Nora Wattie, the assistant medical officer of health for Glasgow. Wattie selected a cross-section of schools to be included in the study for Scotland, with 53 individual schools being selected. The medical officers responsible for each of the schools were asked to fill out a short questionnaire, which would enlighten the Subcommittee as to the current situation. The results showed that within the six rural schools examined in Scotland sanitary towels could be obtained from the school nurse or teacher, but not from the private facility of a slot machine, and there were no bins provided for the disposal of these towels when they needed to be changed.[71] The situation was equally poor in urban schools where, of the 47 examined, 19 had no school facility from which towels could be acquired, and 41 of the 47 schools provided no bins for the disposal of towels.[72] Three of the urban schools reported that girls could dispose of their towels by handing them to the school nurse if needed, but this was hardly an appealing route for the pupils. Moreover, the facilities for changing towels were not conducive to comfort and privacy: 'quite a number of schools, including some large ones with young children of both sexes, have no lavatories

---

[68]'Speech written for Mr Tom Fraser the Under-Secretary of State, 14/4/49', 4.
[69]'Mary', interview by the author, May 20, 2010.
[70]'Supply and Disposal of Sanitary Towels in Schools', *Lancet*, May 28, 1949, 925–7.
[71]'Supply and Disposal of Sanitary Towels in Schools', 926.
[72]Ibid.

with doors that lock'.[73] The members of the Subcommittee were conscious of the failure of the contemporary education system in its provision for adolescent girls and, significantly, they were aware of the damaging effect this could have on day-to-day school-life and especially during activity:

> Wearing a towel too long causes chafing and soreness, with associated discomfort and pain on walking and running: moreover, inability to change when it is known to be necessary sets up an anxiety that may be a panic fear, lest soiling of underwear becomes staining of outer clothes.[74]

In order to be consistently comfortable with their bodies whilst at school it would be necessary for girls to be able to keep clean and dispose of their sanitary towels discreetly. In Helen's memories of her adolescence and menstruation she noted her good fortune that she could go home at lunch to change, as for those girls for whom a home-lunch was not possible menstruation may have been a much more awkward and uncomfortable time:

> A: Well sometimes you might not do the whole day, but I think I would be lucky, could go home for lunch, I could go home and get back. So, different if it was a girl there the whole day –
>
> Q: From further away.
>
> A: Further away. But eh, we could get home and back. It was a rush but we could do it I think, those days, yeah. But yeah, these are the wee changes that are different from that time to –
>
> Q: Now.
>
> A: To now. Aye, you see. But I remember that.[75]

Helen also remembered that physical education was compulsory at all times, even during menstruation: 'Uhuh, you know cause when they came round and that, sometimes it was maybe kinda awkward but eh, you just did the things and I suppose you had them with PE and things like that.'[76] Similarly, Betty, an upper-working-class interviewee from Cardonald near Glasgow, noted that when she was at school in the late 1940s menstruation was not considered to be a valid reason to be excused from physical education:

> A: Well just the old-fashioned thing which I know doesn't really apply was you didn't go swimming when you had your period. You'd always to take a note in to the teacher to say why you weren't, eh why you weren't, ye know, doing swimming. But eh, that wasn't an excuse for like eh –
>
> Q: For anything else, no?
>
> A: No, that wouldn't have been accepted.[77]

---

[73]Ibid.
[74]Ibid., 926–7.
[75]'Helen', interview by the author, May 18, 2010.
[76]Ibid.
[77]'Betty', interview by the author, May 17, 2010.

Whilst this may have showed girls that menstruation was not necessarily a time in which they should view themselves as ill and physically incapable, the facilities within the schools did not seem to be adequate to ensure all girls would be comfortable enough to take part even if they felt well enough to do so. If there were no suitable means or facilities where towels could be changed as regularly as needed, sport participation during menstruation would indeed become uncomfortable and unpleasant. This situation would not set girls up with an appropriate view of the capabilities of their bodies and it probably contributed to the negative way in which some girls viewed their physical capabilities during menstruation, making them much less likely to take part in any activities during this time of the month in their later life. Thus, through a lack of adequate education in both health and sex education within the school environment many of the girls growing up between the 1930s and 1950s in Scotland would have had a low level of knowledge of the workings of their own bodies. The facilities and health education programmes in many Scottish schools were not conducive to a supportive environment for girls in the first years of puberty. This would not have aided the situation of girls who were already unhappy or uncomfortable with their body and its changes, and it is doubtful as to whether it would have enhanced their experiences of physical education.

From the interviews it would seem that active adolescent girls during these years were not acknowledged by officials in Scotland for what they really were: young women. They were seldom provided with facilities that made their daily school experiences more comfortable and encouraged them to be hygienic. This is particularly interesting when we reconsider the fact that at this time officials considered girls' adolescent bodies to be quite fragile, and it was generally suggested that girls at this time of life were going through certain changes which meant they needed to be cared for in the correct way. As noted earlier, for years officials in the Scottish education system had espoused certain attitudes which stressed the unsuitability of vigorous sport for girls in the shape of 'manly' team games or strenuous athletics. Officials seemed to believe that girls' bodies were fragile at this stage of life, as shown by notes in the 1931 curriculum which held in Scotland for some years and stated that girls' competition 'requires careful control' on account of 'physiological' reasoning, suggesting that this guideline was formed from the unquestionable factual findings of medical experts. The idea that violent competitive sport was incompatible with the female form, particularly during adolescence, was still ingrained in the contemporary discursive framework, and this idea had its roots in the medical discourses of the recent past. Paradoxically, officials outlined girls' bodies as being weak and fragile on account of their bodily changes in adolescence, but simultaneously some officials and educators seemed to be oblivious to the presence of these same bodily changes, and failed to provide facilities which might have catered to the needs of girls at this stage in life.

The prevalence of these competing discourses seems to have affected the opinions of some of my interviewees. For example, Margaret H. was a working-class interviewee who grew up in Craigton in south Glasgow in the 1930s and attended Hutchesons' Grammar School by aid of a scholarship. She was a keen swimmer but steered away from what she called 'rough' games like hockey, first because there was a fee required to play it at Hutchesons', which her family could not afford, but also because she was 'too feart!', or too scared, to play hockey. She did, however, enjoy swimming, which experts deemed to be particularly suited to women, and when asked if she worried about hurting herself playing any sports or team games her reply hinted that she was aware of the idea that some sports could damage the young female body but that swimming was not one of them: 'Oh no, I didn't think about that, anyway, I was only swimming and I didn't think you could do much damage there.'[78] In contrast to Margaret H., some other interviewees had such high levels of physical activity in their youth that it is difficult to believe they were worried about damaging their fragile adolescent bodies. For example Christine, a working-class interviewee who grew up in Cardonald in the 1950s, described her young self as 'a good all-rounder at many sports', the most prominent being athletics.[79] It is notable that Christine excelled in sprinting and general athletics as officials considered these to be some of the most 'vigorous' sports, somewhat unsuited to the female body. Evidently Christine did not personally feel that vigorous athletics might damage her feminine functions, and she went on to marry and give birth to three daughters without any complications. Margaret B., who grew up in Yorkshire in the 1950s but spent much of her later life in Stirlingshire, replied with such certainty about her own physical capabilities during adolescence that the official view of girls as universally fragile during this stage of life seems very wide of the mark:

A: When I was an adolescent? … Strong, could conquer the world. Knew that I could improve, there was masses to do, masses to learn. And I wanted to improve my standard of performance in everything.

Q: Were you quite competitive?

A: Yes. Still am. (Laugh)[80]

The interviews suggested that supportive environments both within and, particularly, outside the school environment seemed to nurture the healthy relationships that Margaret B. and Christine had with sport and exercise, and the positive ways in which they viewed the capabilities of their own bodies: they both outlined themselves as being 'naturally sporty'. For girls like Margaret B. and Christine, perhaps the lack of good hygienic facilities at school was not really viewed as an obstacle to their enjoyment as there was no alternative if they really wanted to take part. But for girls like Margaret H., who had never really taken a liking to vigorous exercise initially, enjoyment of sport would hardly have been nurtured as they attempted to negotiate the physiological changes of adolescence within an often unforgiving school environment.

Conclusion

As a result of the various national economic priorities which delayed investment in public and school sports facilities, Scottish PE remained largely unchanged between 1930 and 1960. Nevertheless, gradually from the 1960s onwards a conscious decision was made by official bodies to invest in community and school sport. Consequently a series of financial collaborations between central and local authorities

---

[78]'Margaret H.', interview by the author, May 17, 2010.
[79]'Christine', interview by the author, July 2, 2010.
[80]'Margaret B.', interview by the author, July 27, 2010.

LIVERPOOL JOHN MOORES UNIVERSITY

brought about the establishment of various multi-sports centres and national sporting facilities, which changed the way physical education and community sport interacted, and the scope of opportunity for girls' PE was certainly improved as a result of this.[81] Yet, between 1930 and 1960 there continued to be an absence of sex and health education as an ingrained component of the Scottish curriculum, and the introduction of such teaching in any Scottish school remained at the discretion of the head teacher. From the 1950s representatives from feminine hygiene companies, such as Tampax™, would occasionally be invited to come and speak to groups of adolescent schoolgirls, partly as a sales technique but also for educational purposes. Linda, an interviewee who was born in 1944 and grew up in Uddingston in central Scotland, recalled the Tampax™ representative visiting her own school in 1956: 'In second year we had a talk from the Tampax™ lady and we all just looked at her with great disbelief.'[82] There was thus an option for head teachers to invite experts to the school to speak on these sensitive subjects, but even with this system health instruction would still only be implemented on an ad hoc basis, and this remained the situation for decades.[83]

The general level of ignorance of the inner workings of the female body at this time is striking. There was still no official way through which all girls would get access to useful biological information about their own bodies and until this came about girls would be relying on what they were told by their peers, or, if they were lucky, what their mother explained to them. What is clear is that until girls had enough knowledge about the female body they had no way through which they could decide what their own capabilities were. The school curriculum, which was shaped by what were now largely outdated medical discourses, told them that 'manly competitive or contact sports' such as football, rugby and some athletics were not suitable for girls, on physiological grounds. Understandably, when girls were told by their elders, peers, or by 'experts' that vigorous physical exercise could damage the female body, they did not always have the appropriate factual knowledge about the strength or physical workings of their own bodies to think anything else. Until girls had the biological information at hand to know that competitive sport could not rob them of their 'womanliness', they would be reluctant to get involved.

Officials had to recognise that adolescent girls were really young women who needed to be treated as such, and until then the situation for active girls in school would continue to be far from adequate. This idea of the lack of understanding of the female body and appreciation of this situation can hopefully go some way in helping our understandings of women's relationships with their own bodies and how this affected female participation in sport. We should appreciate that throughout the mid-twentieth century the official school environment often failed to adequately nurture young female bodies and cater for girls to allow them to participate comfortably in sport to the best of their ability. Those girls who viewed themselves as 'sporty' were often encouraged by an individual outside school, such as a father or brother, or by a particularly enthusiastic PE teacher who had access to good sports facilities and could nurture their talent. But for those who had been schooled

---

[81]See for example NAS, ED27 375, Assistance for Sport: Prototype Sports Centre, 1968–70, *Bellahouston Sport Centre*.

[82]'Linda', interview by the author, October 25, 2010.

[83]Davidson and Davis, '"This Thorniest of Problems"', 244.

in the belief that vigorous sports were unsuitable for girls, there was little scope for them to develop their knowledge in this area without personally pushing the boundaries of their own capabilities. Yet, fear of damaging their bodies would have been enough to stop many girls from venturing beyond what was officially recommended and testing the limits of their bodies. We can perhaps see more clearly why the 'sportswoman' was a difficult concept for society to grasp and why it was so important that there were some determined young women, such as Christine and Margaret B., who tested the physical capabilities of their bodies and helped to show their communities that the female body and sport were highly compatible.

Who killed schoolgirl cricket? The Women's Cricket Association and the death of an opportunity, 1945–1960[1]

Rafaelle Nicholson

History, Queen Mary, University of London, London, UK

This article examines the reasons behind the decline of schoolgirl cricket in the years between 1945 and 1960. It considers the impact of the Education Act 1944 and 'secondary education for all' on girls' physical education in general, focusing on why certain sports, in particular cricket, were not widely introduced into the new secondary modern and grammar schools. The outreach programme of the Women's Cricket Association, the governing body of women's cricket, to these new schools is considered alongside the problem of equipment and pitch shortages. Ultimately, blame for schoolgirl cricket's failure to become entrenched within the English education system is placed on the attitudes of teachers and Local Education Authorities towards girls' cricket at this time; they considered the sport unsuitable for female pupils. Overall, the article serves as a historical case study of gendered physical education in action.

In the 1970s the Sports Council declared that women's cricket, as a sport, was 'dying'.[2] By 1970 only 66 clubs were affiliated to the governing body of the sport, the Women's Cricket Association (WCA), compared with 200 in 1955. A key factor in this decline was the failure of the WCA to revitalise its membership in the post-war period by attracting young members: at its lowest point, just 46 schools were affiliated.[3] Evidently, cricket for schoolgirls had not become a popular choice of activity.

It has become a truism in research on physical education (PE) to suggest that the British system has historically sustained and reproduced ideologies of sexual difference. Sheila Scraton is a key proponent of this view:

Schools as important institutions serve to reproduce the status quo in relation to the capitalist mode of production and male–female power relations.... Physical education as an aspect of schooling fits into this process both in terms of its relationship to a

---

[1] I thank Peter Catterall for his helpful comments on an earlier draft of this article.
[2] Jack Williams, 'Cricket', in *Sport in Britain: A Social History*, ed. Tony Mason (Cambridge: Cambridge University Press, 1989), 141.
[3] Women's Cricket Association, 'Yearbook 1955' and 'Yearbook 1970', Women's Cricket Associates, http://www.womenscrickethistory.org/ (accessed January 27, 2012).

sexual division of leisure in society and the reinforcement of patriarchal power relations.[4]

More recent work on the subject has reinforced this argument.[5] The inclusion of team games in the curriculum, in particular, has been seen as a key way of encouraging acceptable 'feminine' behaviour, by 'limiting girls' access to those sports which stressed endurance, strength or physical contact'.[6] Thus, within educational institutions, girls have been encouraged to participate in netball and hockey, whilst football and rugby have remained masculine domains.

However, despite the prevailing acceptance of this view, many of its premises are based on generalisations, without detailed historical evidence to support their conclusions. Hargreaves's history of women's sport, for example, only briefly considers schoolgirl games, and her accounts rely heavily on a few oral history reminiscences and official pronouncements by the Board (later Ministry) of Education.[7] Her conclusions are thus subject to sampling error and tend towards an oversimplification of the varied experiences of those participating in PE in the interwar and postwar period. More general histories of sport in the UK have focused almost exclusively on the experiences of sport in adulthood; Holt and Mason state simply that '[c]omprehensive education did not make sport a priority'.[8]

There has been some relevant work conducted on PE in state schools in the interwar period. McIntosh, Welshman and Skillen have all highlighted the increasing involvement of the Board of Education in PE in the years from 1900.[9] Attempts were made in these years to standardise provision of PE in the state sector, through the introduction of syllabi and the passing of legislation including the Physical Training and Recreation Act of 1937, which sought to provide for the establishment of centres to encourage physical recreation. Lessons which had originally centred largely on military drill were becoming much more focused on recreative aspects and the playing of team games. However, prior to the war most working-class girls left school at 14, and it was recognised that facilities and finances, equipment and pitches were extremely limited. Welshman highlights 'the great gulf that could exist between rhetoric and reality' up to 1939.[10]

---

[4]Sheila Scraton, *Shaping up to Womanhood: Gender and Girls' Physical Education* (Milton Keynes: Open University Press, 1992), 18.

[5]See for example Jennifer Hargreaves, *Sporting Females: Critical Issues in the History and Sociology of Women's Sports* (London: Routledge, 1994), and Dawn Penney and John Evans (eds.), *Gender and Physical Education: Contemporary Issues and Future Directions* (London: Routledge, 2002).

[6]Scraton, *Shaping up to Womanhood*, 28.

[7]Hargreaves, *Sporting Females*, 120–2, 152–4.

[8]Richard Holt and Tony Mason, *Sport in Britain, 1945–2000* (Oxford: Oxford University Press, 2000), 17.

[9]Peter McIntosh, *Physical Education in England since 1800* (London: Camelot Press, 1952); John Welshman, 'Physical Culture and Sport in British Schools, 1900–40', *International Journal of the History of Sport* 15, no. 1 (1998): 71; John Welshman, 'Physical Education and the School Medical Service in England and Wales, 1907–39', *Social History of Medicine* 9, no. 1 (1996): 47; Fiona Skillen, '"A Sound System of Physical Training": The Development of PE in Interwar Scotland', *History of Education* 38, no. 3 (2009): 406.

[10]Welshman, 'PE and the School Medical Service': 48.

Much less has been written on the post-1944 Education Act period.[11] In order to substantiate the claim that PE is inherently gendered as a result of its historical development, more in-depth studies of these years are necessary. The discussion that follows considers PE in the immediate postwar period in some detail, with a focus on the Women's Cricket Association. It was in these years that those in authority experienced their first opportunity to introduce PE at secondary level to a mass market. The 1944 Education Act stated:

> It shall be the duty of every local education authority to secure that there are adequate facilities for recreation and social and physical training, and for that purpose a local education authority may establish, maintain and manage camps, holiday classes, playing fields, play centres, playgrounds, gymnasiums, and swimming baths.[12]

For the first time, physical education provision became an obligatory responsibility of local education authorities (LEAs); this differed from the permissive legislation of the interwar years. There was therefore huge potential to introduce particular sports to the influx of girls (and boys) coming into secondary schools. Additionally, because many of the new secondary schools were coeducational, there was an unprecedented opportunity to introduce sports which had previously only been played at single-sex boys' schools to their female classmates. This was a key moment if schoolgirl cricket was ever to become entrenched within the English education system.

This article seeks to understand why, even in a period of 'secondary education for all', this did not occur. It asks why, right from the onset of the tripartite system, some sports were encouraged above others in the school curriculum for girls, and why some, like cricket, were always excluded from consideration. In doing so, it builds on the work of those like Skillen who have highlighted the focus on gymnastics, hockey, netball and swimming in interwar syllabi for girls as a result of these activities being seen as 'appropriate and suitable for young sportswomen' due to the restraints they placed upon them.[13] Here, cricket for girls is used as a case study. It provides an interesting example because, unlike football and rugby, it is a non-contact sport and not overtly aggressive, or 'masculine'. Indeed, those in the WCA had always drawn attention to its graceful and 'feminine' aspects.[14] It had also long been played by women: the first recorded match dated back to 1745, and middle-class females had increasingly taken up the sport during the nineteenth century.[15] Why, therefore, was the opportunity to introduce cricket to a new market, working-class girls, squandered so comprehensively? Was it, as might be claimed, a case of girls themselves rejecting the sport, or did an untapped demand for girls' cricket exist?

The first section considers the established argument that the WCA, the governing body of women's cricket, can be blamed for the decline of schoolgirl cricket

---

[11]Exceptions are McIntosh, *Physical Education in England*, and Sheila Fletcher, *Women First: The Female Tradition in English Physical Education* (London: Athlone Press, 1984).

[12]*Education Act 1944*, 7 and 8 Geo 6 c. 31 (London: HMSO), s.53(1).

[13]Skillen, "A Sound System of Physical Training", 413.

[14]See for example Marjorie Pollard, *Cricket for Women and Girls* (London: Hutchinson, 1934), 13–14, 65.

[15]Kathleen McCrone, *Sport and the Physical Emancipation of English Women* (London: Routledge, 1988), Chapter 5.

because of its supposed elitism. The attitudes of the organisation, as demonstrated in Association minutes and the WCA's official magazine, will be considered along-side the school affiliation figures that have been used to indict them. The second section considers the alternative argument that facilities within state schools were insufficient for school cricket to ever be a viable option in the new secondary modern schools, utilising official Ministry of Education pronouncements on and investigations into PE during this period. It is argued that cricket was not in fact outside the financial and spatial remit of the secondary modern school. Ultimately, the final section seeks to demonstrate, through the combined use of Ministry of Education and WCA documentation, that official attitudes to schoolgirl cricket remained hostile. The article indicates the need to consider attitudes to PE in schools from the perspective of both government and governing body, something which has not been done previously. It supports the argument that PE in schools helped perpet-uate traditional gender roles, demonstrating the culpability of those within education in neglecting to promote cricket for girls, and providing a key case study approach to understanding the gendered history of PE within the English system.

'School-leavers constitute the Suez Canal for the WCA'

The WCA had been formed in 1926 by a group of female hockey players who wanted a team game to play in the summer months, and their efforts in the years up to 1939 had enabled cricket for women to take off on a national scale. By 1938 the Association had grown into a governing body with 20 county associations, 105 clubs and 82 schools affiliated. International women's cricket had been initiated, with the WCA sending a team to Australia and New Zealand in 1934–1935, and a return visit being made by the Australians in 1937. A moderate amount of press coverage and public interest had been attracted through the WCA's publicity efforts, including the production of their own cricket film, and some male county cricketing authorities had proved keen to host annual representative matches.[16] There was much to be proud of.

In the years before 1939, however, cricket had been concentrated in large female public schools like Roedean, St Leonard's and Wycombe Abbey, as well as the High Schools run by the Girls Public Day School Trust (GPDST): schools which were pioneers in promoting physical activity for women.[17] In the state sector, the Board of Education recommended netball and rounders as the chief school games for girls. An official policy document in 1927 stated that: 'Hockey and lacrosse do not as a rule come within the scope of senior elementary school classes owing to the amount of time required to master the difficulties of technique, the expense of a specially prepared grass surface, and the provision of sufficiently good equipment. Cricket presents even greater difficulties … unless suitable conditions are available, the games are not worth attempting because they cannot be played satisfactorily.'[18]

Thus, of the 82 schools affiliated to the WCA in 1938, 63 or approximately 75% were independent schools; only 19 were wholly state-maintained. This has led

---

[16]See Jack Williams, *Cricket and England: A Social and Cultural History of the Interwar Years* (London: Frank Cass, 1999), 92–111.

[17]McCrone, *Sport and the Physical Emancipation of English Women*, 60–90.

[18]Board of Education, *Supplement to 1919 Syllabus of Physical Training for Older Girls* (London: HMSO, 1927), 33.

some historians to accuse the WCA of elitism and of stifling its own development. Jack Williams's argument is that:

> Women's cricket was controlled by those from economically privileged groups.... [The WCA] tried to organise the women's game in accordance with the values of men's cricket clubs for those from the wealthier classes in the south of England.[19]

Additionally, Martin Francis has asserted that '[w]omen's cricket ... failed to attract interest outside the products of a few elite private schools'.[20] These explanations do not apparently allow for any development of cricket in the new secondary modern schools. Not only, according to these interpretations, was the WCA an elitist organisation, but state school girls themselves showed no interest in the sport. It is necessary to challenge these kinds of statement not just because of their factual inaccuracy, but because they perpetuate the sense that cricket does not belong in state schools – a factor that has played no small part in its decline as a school sport over the past half-century.[21]

In fact, a detailed examination of the ways in which the WCA reacted to the new system of 'secondary education for all' very quickly reveals its members to have been exceptionally concerned to increase school affiliations and thereby inject new blood into their association. During their 1952 AGM, it was recognised that 'the present danger lay in being content to remain in the same old rut.... More coaching facilities were needed for young people wishing to learn the game.'[22] In 1947 a Schools Sub-Committee was formed:

> ... the first object should be to form groups of schoolgirl cricketers in as many areas as possible. Miss [Elizabeth] Riley [a Territorial Representative for the East Territory and a Kent player] suggested that arrangements might be made for prominent members of the WCA to visit all affiliated, and any possible non-affiliated schools, to speak to the Games Mistresses and girls, if possible, and distribute suitable WCA literature, not forgetting the film.[23]

Letters were sent to all schools which had been affiliated pre-war inviting re-affiliation, and to all County Secretaries recommending the formation of groups of schoolgirl cricketers and the organisation of school cricket rallies to provide group coaching. An 'advantages of membership' leaflet was distributed which cited coaching facilities, reduced admission to territorial and international women's matches, free literature and the WCA's annual festival of cricket, Colwall Cricket Week, as

---

[19]Jack Williams, *Cricket and England*, 100.

[20]Martin Francis, 'Leisure and Popular Culture', in *Women in Twentieth-Century Britain*, ed. Ina Zweiniger-Bargielowska (Harlow: Longman, 2001), 237.

[21]On the decline of cricket in state schools, see the *Telegraph*, May 20, 2010. There is evidence that state school teachers have been reluctant to introduce cricket even among male pupils due to concerns about its unsuitability in this context. See for example *School Sport Magazine*, July 1976.

[22]Women's Cricket Association, 'Yearbook 1952: AGM minutes', Women's Cricket Associates, http://www.womenscrickethistory.org/ (accessed January 27, 2012).

[23]WCA Executive Committee minutes, November 14, 1947, WCA Archive, Lancashire.

reasons why schools should affiliate to the WCA.[24] An annual 'Holiday Coaching Week' was instituted, targeting young players, and partly financed by the WCA itself. In conjunction with the Central Council of Physical Recreation, WCA volunteers ran numerous coaching courses around the country. A key motivating factor for schools to affiliate was the significantly reduced annual affiliation fee, which in 1945 was just five shillings per school and two shillings and sixpence for schoolgirls, compared with £5 for an adult member of an affiliated club.[25] Liaising with teaching staff was also an important part of the WCA's strategy: in 1950 they stated that their policy 'had been that of pleading with colleges, Physical Training Organisers and Headmistresses to include cricket in their curricula. Where it has been possible, cricket has been included.'[26]

The minutes of grassroots women's cricket clubs indicate that local-level initiatives were also being pursued. The Redoubtables Women's Cricket Club, based in Surrey and with an average membership of 25, provides a good example of how women's clubs were seeking to engage with schoolgirls in their localities. The members paid for Joan Hawes, a promising youngster (who went on to play for England) to attend Cricket Week in 1952, and in 1959 they paid for two junior club members to attend a Surrey coaching course. In 1957 they lent their ground at Beddington Park to Surrey WCA for the County Schoolgirl Trials, without charge. They also regularly wrote to all schools in Surrey, requesting the names of girls interested in cricket who would be leaving at the end of the school year.[27] Redoubtables were a well-off club located in an affluent area, and a lack of research into grassroots women's cricket means it is not yet possible to make conclusions about how typical their activities may have been. Nonetheless, the fact that they were following WCA directives suggests that their efforts were probably commonly replicated elsewhere around the country.

Some of the WCA's resources were, it must be admitted, concentrated in continued outreach to the public schools, as evidenced by their magazines, which report WCA visits during the 1950s in an attempt to encourage those with a long-established tradition to remain enthusiastic about their cricket. Both Cheltenham Ladies' College and Wycombe Abbey, for example, entertained the Australian players to lunch during their 1951 tour 'and subsequently followed their fortunes at the second and final test matches at Worcester and the Oval with great interest'.[28] But what was new about the postwar period, and particularly striking, was the fact that efforts were no longer exclusively focused on the public or even the older grammar schools. In *Women's Cricket* magazine, the official magazine of the WCA, the organisers of central schoolgirl coaching sessions reported numerous successes in attracting girls from secondary modern schools to attend. Kent's scheme of 1948

---

[24]Colwall is a village in Herefordshire. The WCA's Cricket Week was held there because this was where the founders of the Association had been holidaying when they made the decision to form the WCA; the village was referred to as the 'birthplace' of women's cricket.

[25]Women's Cricket Association, 'Yearbook 1946: WCA Rules', Women's Cricket Associates, http://www.womenscrickethistory.org/ (accessed January 27, 2012).

[26]WCA Executive Committee minutes, December 9, 1950, WCA Archive, Lancashire.

[27]Redoubtables AGM and Executive Committee minutes, 1945–60, private collection, Wallington, Surrey.

[28]*Cheltenham Ladies College Magazine*, 1951, 91. *Wycombe Abbey Gazette*, December 1951, 86.

attracted 123 girls from local secondary modern and grammar schools. Similarly Warwickshire's 1949 coaching session attracted 83 girls after typed circulars were sent to all local secondary modern and grammar schools. In Nottinghamshire, the 1950 Schoolgirls' Coaching Scheme was open to girls from Nottingham's grammar and private schools, but by 1951 it included two secondary modern schools.[29] It is difficult to know what the exact make-up of these events would have been but it does show at least some level of interest from secondary modern schools where the opportunity to play cricket was available.

Members of the Physical Education Inspectorate established at the Ministry of Education after the war were quick to blame governing bodies for a lack of engagement with schools, arguing that these bodies were often to forge links between their own activities and those occurring within education. In 1961, the Inspectorate agreed

> that the shortage of facilities played into the hands of those people (including governing bodies of sport) who were only interested in using the most able players.... Governing bodies of sport were not interested ... in this [less able] section, the schools' population.[30]

Certainly in the case of the WCA this accusation is patently untrue and unfair. All coaching courses were open to absolute beginners: adult female cricketers were attempting outreach, regardless of ability.

The WCA were quite clear as to why schoolgirl outreach was such an important priority. An August 1956 editorial of *Women's Cricket* magazine suggested that:

> School-leavers constitute the Suez Canal for the WCA. They are our life-blood and vital to us if we are to survive ... probably our biggest liability is the relatively small entry of school-leavers into the clubs.... What can we do more to encourage the younger members? ... We must consider the formation and organisation of After-School clubs, junior sections, reduced club affiliation fees for youngsters, suitable publicity, energetic and enthusiastic physical education staff and many other possible remedies. And we must act.[31]

Given earlier events of that year, this reference to the Suez Canal is rather amusing in retrospect. Nonetheless, quotations like this one absolutely support the fact that the WCA were, as a whole, very concerned with the reinvigoration of their membership and were willing to go to great lengths to ensure that new members were made welcome.

Yet, overall, how successful were these efforts at engagement with the new state secondary schools? One measure of success must surely be the WCA's school affiliation figures for the postwar years. These do seem to suggest only limited success at outreach.

As can be seen from Table 1, though grammar school affiliations had increased by 1960, there continued to be only tiny numbers of comprehensive schools affiliated, and no secondary modern schools at all. The figures for grammar schools

---

[29] *Women's Cricket*, May 29, 1948, August 20, 1949, June 14, 1951.
[30] PE Inspectorate meeting, January 9 and 10, 1961, ED 118/16, National Archives, Public Record Office, Kew (hereafter TNA: PRO).
[31] *Women's Cricket*, 31 August, 1956.

Table 1. Schools affiliated to the WCA in 1950 and 1960.

Year	Total	Independent schools	Grammar schools	Secondary moderns	Technical schools	Comprehensives	Other
1950	82	38	33	0	1	0	10[a]
1960	87	33	43	0	0	2	9[b]

Notes: [a]This includ[es ...] [d]irect-grant schools, one voluntary-aided school and two convent schools. [b]This includes th[ree ...]ST schools and two convent schools. Source: These data are taken from the WCA's 'Year[book ...]', Women's Cricket Associates, http://www.womenscrickethistory.org/ (accessed January 27[...]

[...]: the number had risen from 33 in 1950 to 43 in 1960. However, many [...] were older grammar schools, generally located in more affluent areas, some [...]ich had merely continued their pre-war affiliations.[32] This compared unfavour-[...] with other sports. By 1950, the All England Women's Hockey Association had [...]86 school affiliations (compared with 695 schools in 1939), many of which were secondary modern schools.[33] The Northumberland representative of the All England Netball Association reported that in 1939 a mere 10 schools had been affiliated, but by 1951 the figures were 14 grammar schools and 61 secondary modern schools. This appears to have been fairly typical.[34] If, as I have been arguing here, WCA efforts were so exhaustive, why were their attempts to increase state school affiliations such a failure? The concluding two sections of the article will address this question.

'In many Modern Schools the work is crippled because of the poor facilities'

The educational policy of the Attlee governments has recently been described as 'the most important gap in Labour's egalitarianism';[35] from their beginnings, the new secondary modern schools were often hampered by a lack of funds, and a key element of this was PE. The 1944 Education Act was supposed to ensure that no schools were without a playing field, but many school buildings remained out of date. John Newsom's *The Education of Girls*, published in 1948, reported on the ways in which the English education system differentiated between boys and girls, and made recommendations regarding the future of female secondary education. His report touched on the problem of PE, stating:

> Many of these [secondary modern] schools have no playing space other than the tar-mac of the playground, the girls never handle a tennis racquet or a hockey stick…. [They spend] an hour in the playground practising netball, under difficulties since some 200 other girls are milling around in various forms of unorganized play and a good deal of shouting and laughter.[36]

---

[32]At least 23 were grammar schools dating from before 1945. Nine had been affiliated to the WCA before the war.

[33]'AEWHA Report, 1950', ED 169/36, TNA: PRO.

[34]All England Netball Association, *The Silver Jubilee Book: Netball 1901–1951* (Manchester: AENA, 1951), 15–25.

[35]Paul Addison, *No Turning Back: The Peacetime Revolutions of Post-War Britain* (Oxford: Oxford University Press, 2010), 40.

[36]John Newsom, *The Education of Girls* (London: Faber & Faber, 1948), 89–91.

There were two other key problems. First, it was recognised that the limited amount of time given to PE in schools – often just tw[o] 30-minute periods a week – rendered the development of the skills needed for ... games out of reach.[37] Additionally, there remained a severely limited suppl[y] [of] specialist teachers in both grammar and modern schools. A sample of staffing ... PE taken from eight counties and 10 boroughs in April 1949 uncovered an ave[rage] teaching shortfall of 64% and 61.5% in the grammar and modern schools resp... [38] The situation did improve over time. However, the Newsom Report of 196[3] found that less than a third of the schools sampled had playing field provision ... the standard prescribed by regulations' and '[m]any lacked an adequate gymn...[39]

The Ministry of Education did not produce any new PE s... schools in this period. By default, therefore, the new schools ... secondary Board of Education's *Syllabus of Physical Training for Schools*, ... the 1933 large demand after 1945 and was reprinted in 1949 unaltered.[40] This ... still in girls: for

> *Netball* has proved itself a remarkably suitable game for playgrounds.... *Shinty,* ball, *Touch and Pass*, *Rugby touch*, *Rounders* and *Stoolball* are team games can be brought to a high pitch of skill, and if played well, will provide a u... foundation for any games the girls may take up on leaving school. *Cricket* prese... considerable difficulties owing to the cost of good pitches. It may be possible ... certain schools to secure both the services of a teacher who is a first class coach and the right facilities for play, but unless suitable conditions are available, the game should not be attempted. *Lacrosse* with its difficult preliminary technique and expensive equipment does not yet come within the scope of elementary schools. *Hockey* is being played with increasing success in certain districts where sufficient level pitches can be secured.[41]

In the years after 1945, according to the Physical Education Inspectorate, netball and rounders remained important school games for girls, but hockey and tennis also became increasingly widespread. Given the above conditions, it might be argued that any form of cricket continued to be almost impossible: the Board of Education had implied that it required a school to pay for both new equipment and the upkeep of a pitch. The argument is not this straightforward, however. First, it appears that where money was available for new PE facilities it was often disproportionately allocated to facilities for boys. A PE Inspectorate Memorandum dated 2 April 1953 stated: 'In many Modern Schools the work is crippled because of the poor facilities, and in mixed schools the situation is usually worse.... Very often *the girls have no playing field*.'[42] Another memorandum from the same year on the situation in the South of England demonstrated that this was becoming a concern by including a category of 'equal consideration [for] boys and girls' in measurement of new

---

[37]Memo, 'Physical Education in Secondary Modern Schools', April 2, 1953, ED 158/115, TNA: PRO.

[38]Memo, 'Supply of Specialist Teachers in Grammar and Modern Schools', March 1951, ED 158/114, TNA: PRO.

[39]*Newsom Report* (London: HMSO, 1963), Chapter 17.

[40]PE Inspectorate meeting, April 24 and 25, 1947, ED 158/114, TNA: PRO.

[41]Board of Education, *Syllabus of Physical Training for Schools* (London: HMSO, 1933; reprinted 1949), 39. Emphasis in the original.

[42]Memo, 'Physical Education in Secondary Schools', April 2, 1953, ED 158/115, TNA: PRO. My italics.

gymnasia. In this case, it was found that Wimbourne County Secondary Modern in Dorset did not have equal pro... on (though the other 10 schools surveyed stated that they did). Newsom also... his 1963 Report recognised that 'Mary ... is a the typical secondary mo...hn to play for a school team ... because games play a good deal less likely ... than for boys.... There are in fact in the sample roughly less important part girls who play regularly for a school team.'[43] twice as many b...ever took precedence. The PE Inspectorate found that in 1959

Second, li...ogramme for girls always included gymnastics, often involved that certai...prised hockey, netball, tennis and swimming 'where possible'. Ath- the typ...sual in girls' schools and other activities were 'occasional'; cricket danc...n mentioned by name. The Inspectorate seemed to agree that this order le...nce was advisable, commenting: 'The following ought to be included in ...year – gymnastics, dance, hockey or lacrosse, swimming ... gymnastics ...ance ... should be a constant factor in the programme.... It is difficult to ...ow how far girls really enjoy athletics.'[44] Another priority was swimming; the minutes of the Inspectorate indicate a push in the postwar years to make this an activity available to all secondary school children, despite the obvious difficulties with having to travel to pools away from school premises. This had been a focus pre-war too: in the 1933 Syllabus, the Board of Education stated that their aim was for 'every school ... [to] make provision for the inclusion of this subject in its curriculum'.[45] Swimming pool usage, the upkeep of hockey pitches, new tennis courts and the corresponding equipment required were not cheap, but schools and education authorities were prepared to spend money on them, or at the very least pay to hire out the facilities at local parks. Additionally McIntosh reports that it was in these years that many LEAs introduced 'outdoor activities such as canoeing, sailing, climbing and outdoor adventure in general ... for the first time'.[46]

Cricket was therefore not necessarily beyond the budgetary constraints of state secondary schools. Indeed, it was being played and encouraged at some secondary modern schools. Girls at the Hayward School, Bolton, attended joint practices on the pitch they shared with the neighbouring technical and grammar schools. Girls from all three of these schools were invited to join a team which regularly played after school hours. Eventually the headmistress agreed to include cricket in the games curriculum of the school.[47] Some secondary modern schools could even offer facilities to local clubs that were struggling for resources. At Dorchester Secondary Modern School in 1955 the newly formed Dorchester Women's Cricket Club agreed to hold its practices on school premises, due largely to the fact that its Secretary was a teacher at the school. A similar situation occurred with Norfolk WCA, who used the Secondary Modern School at Fakenham for meetings.[48] A pitch was not necessarily a requirement, either. One schoolgirl reported on what could be achieved even with scarce resources, if the teaching staff were willing to cooperate:

---

[43]*Newsom Report*, Chapter 22.

[44]PE Inspectorate meeting, September 21 and 22, 1959, ED 118/16, TNA: PRO.

[45]Board of Education, *Syllabus of Physical Training*, 63.

[46]McIntosh, *Physical Education in England*, 264.

[47]*Women's Cricket*, May 1, 1959.

[48]Ibid., June 10, 1955 and May 14, 1954.

I was lucky enough to be at a school which is affiliated to the WCA. The headmistress is vice-chairman of the association and takes a keen interest in games. Girls at our school have one cricket lesson a week in their second year. They are taught first of all to field and bowl, using a hard ball.... This is then followed by mass coaching in all the basic batting strokes.[49]

Her school did not possess its own pitch but was able to introduce cricket to its pupils nonetheless. Ultimately, as the WCA indicated in its engagement with local schools that did not possess pitches, a lot could be achieved if teaching staff were enthusiastic and prepared to improvise with less than ideal equipment. As one WCA member wrote, '[i]f a school has space to play rounders, it should be possible to play cricket bat and ball games in the same area. Why not rounders with a cricket bat and ball and a pitched ball!'[50]

Cricket was in fact becoming much more readily available to boys in state schools, often in the same schools attended by girls, thanks to effective liaison between the Marylebone Cricket Club (MCC, the governing body of men's cricket in Britain) and the LEAs. There was some recognition in the years after the war that the way to improve the standard of English Test players was to provide better facilities for boys, particularly those at state schools. Thus in 1948, following the 4–0 Ashes defeat which had been dogged by selection issues, the MCC announced an enquiry into youth cricket. Chaired by H.S. Altham, treasurer and later president of the MCC, the committee's remit was 'to examine the problems concerned with the learning and playing of cricket by the youth of the country between the age of eleven and the time of their entry into National Service', and 'to consider how best to foster their enthusiasm for our national game by providing them with wider opportunities for reaping its benefits'.[51] A whole host of bodies were represented, among them the WCA by the England captain Molly Hide. This was the first time women had ever been represented on an MCC committee.

In 1950 the committee's recommendations were published. Their main proposal was the establishment of a national organisation, controlled by the MCC, to coordinate coaching around the country, through new Area Youth Cricket Councils.[52] Two years later, the MCC Youth Cricket Association was formed and by 1957, 34 Area Youth Councils had been established, covering every first-class county and working in collaboration with their LEAs.[53] This work has been described by Holt and Mason as an 'innovation' in postwar British sport.[54]

Crucially, the remit of the committee was to consider the situation for boys *and girls* and in its concluding remarks the report stated:

We understand that this is the first time that a body of so widely representative a nature has been called together by the MCC, and we wish to record our great satisfaction in the fact that at no stage was any real divergence of view apparent, despite the

---

[49]John St John, ed., *The MCC Book for the Young Cricketer* (London: Naldrett Press, 1951), 52.

[50]*Women's Cricket*, September 5, 1958.

[51]Marylebone Cricket Club, *Report of the Cricket Enquiry Committee* (London: MCC, 1950), 1.

[52]Ibid., 12.

[53]Derek Birley, *A Social History of English Cricket* (London: Aurum Press, 1999; reprinted 2003), 278.

[54]Holt and Mason, *Sport in Britain*, 21.

variety and complexity of the issues involved, and the many interests affected. This unanimity appears to us to emphasise the general recognition of the urgency of the problem and of the widespread desire to try and find a solution.[55]

By 1956, 112 out of 325 secondary modern schools in London were coeducational, a situation being replicated across the country in the postwar period.[56] There was therefore clearly a market for the introduction of cricket into these new mixed schools, where it could be played by both boys and girls in a way that maximised efficient use of resources. Indeed, four coeducational schools were affiliated to the WCA in 1960, all of which encouraged the sport for both male and female pupils. Yet the majority of affiliated state schools were single-sex, with the implication that most coeducational state schools where boys played cricket had not introduced it for girls.[57] The problem was that in practice, while cricket for boys was perceived as important, there was still only a limited recognition – as we have already seen – that girls might also want to play while at state schools. By 1955 only three counties had invited female representatives to take part in their Youth Advisory Committees.[58] Despite WCA efforts, two of these committees had actively refused to appoint women, and the others do not appear to have responded to WCA requests.[59] Cricket for boys was therefore able to expand, while it remained difficult for girls to participate.

It appears that a simple lack of facilities does not explain the absence of school-girl cricket from state-maintained schools in this period. In fact, we must look in more detail at the attitudes of both teachers and LEAs to discover why certain sports were encouraged above others. The next section examines these two groups in greater depth.

'Girls will not enjoy a game in which they have neither aptitude nor interest'

Given the lack of guidance from central government about precisely which sports should be encouraged at secondary level in the years after 1945, the attitudes of individual teachers and LEAs were often crucial in determining what, in practice, occurred during PE lessons. By considering WCA comments on the attitudes of these groups to schoolgirl cricket alongside the statements teachers and LEAs them-selves made, it is possible to ascertain why cricket was not a favoured sport for girls. The evidence produced below supports the argument that PE developed after the war in a way which reinforced and reproduced traditional gender roles.

Expenditure by LEAs on recreation and physical training increased from £2,239,000 in 1946–1947 to £3,601,000 in 1950–1951; by 1960, a government

---

[55]MCC, *Report of the Cricket Enquiry Committee*, 23.

[56]*Directory of Modern Secondary Schools 1956* (London: School Government Publishing Company, 1956), 35–46.

[57]By 1960 at least 36 of the state schools affiliated to the WCA were single-sex. See Women's Cricket Association, 'Yearbook 1960', Women's Cricket Associates, http://www.womenscrickethistory.org/ (accessed January 27, 2012).

[58]These were Yorkshire, Sussex and Surrey. See *Women's Cricket*, May 4, 1951.

[59]WCA Executive Committee minutes, October 27, 1950 and December 9, 1950, WCA Archive, Lancashire.

report indicated that this was a long-term trend, as spending was 50% greater in this area than it had been in 1945.[60] The newly created Ministry of Education offered grants towards the salaries of national coaches in sport, as well as continuing to grant-aid voluntary youth organisations and work closely with the Central Council of Physical Recreation. For example, by 1952 the Ministry had awarded £2896 to the Amateur Athletics Association, £1413 to the Lawn Tennis Association, and £410 to the All England Women's Hockey Association.[61] The Ministry also offered grants for coaching, and to specific schools for the purchase of equipment to be used in PE lessons.

Yet the Ministry does not appear to have been favourably disposed to the WCA as a body. In 1948 the WCA applied for funding for five part-time coaches to be spread over the country, each to receive a salary of £80 a year and visit affiliated and non-affiliated schools during the summer months, while organising indoor coaching during the winter. But the application was turned down and the WCA was forced to evolve an independent scheme of its own, establishing a panel of unpaid, volunteer coaches.[62] WCA minutes also report examples of education authorities turning down applications for grants made by schools to purchase cricketing equipment. They appear to have felt that the money would be better spent elsewhere.[63] A prevailing negative attitude is reinforced by a 1953 report in *Women's Cricket* that some female teachers considered it unwise to mention their background in cricket when applying for teaching jobs: 'it isn't safe', one was quoted as saying, '[e]ducation authorities don't like it'.[64] Most LEAs appear to have been reluctant to endorse cricket for girls in the schools in their localities.

At times, the PE Inspectorate implied that there was no point spending money on cricket; girls were only interested in certain games, and cricket was not one of them. In 1959 they stated:

> Interest in field games is certainly not as strong as it used to be, and Saturday matches are becoming more and more unpopular with girls who live in a society which has 'Saturday off'.... Tennis and badminton are very popular and very fashionable.[65]

This, however, was a self-perpetuating argument. If girls were not offered cricket while at school, they did not have any opportunity to develop an interest and the sport did not become 'fashionable' in the same way that tennis did. Besides, it is clear that there was a huge untapped market of interest in the sport. Netta Rheinberg, the editor of *Women's Cricket*, wrote in a 1950 editorial that

> the core of my correspondence ... is made up of letters from schoolgirls, or youngsters just out of school, who wish to play cricket. Some have watched a lot of cricket;

---

[60]Ministry of Education, *The Youth Service in England and Wales* (London: HMSO, 1960), 8.
[61]PE Inspectorate meeting, December 18 and 19, 1952, ED 158/15, TNA: PRO.
[62]WCA Executive Committee minutes, January 17, 1948 and May 21, 1948, WCA Archive, Lancashire.
[63]See for example WCA Executive Committee minutes, June 21, 1948, WCA Archive, Lancashire.
[64]*Women's Cricket*, April 24, 1953.
[65]PE Inspectorate meeting, December 21 and 22, 1959, ED 118/16, TNA: PRO.

some have played a bit with their brothers; some not even that – they are just 'keen' to play England's national summer game.[66]

Teachers also wrote to the magazine indicating that their pupils were favourably disposed to cricket when they had the opportunity to play. Miss Taylor, of Stone-house Secondary Modern School in Gloucestershire, found that girls were 'extremely keen and practice every lunch hour … the girls have thoroughly enjoyed all the matches they played … I can fully recommend [cricket in these schools]'.[67] The fact that schoolgirls attended the WCA's central coaching sessions out of school hours, where these were offered, indicates a good level of interest.

An enthusiasm felt by teachers for cricket was often the difference between a school introducing it to its pupils and bypassing it completely. Unfortunately for the WCA, there appears to have been widespread teacher hostility to schoolgirl cricket in these years. Girls regularly wrote to *Women's Cricket* magazine complaining that, for example, '[o]ur school does not play cricket in the summer because our head-mistress considers the game unladylike'.[68] In 1958 an article was published in the *Illustrated Leicester Chronicle*, printing the responses of several headmistresses to the question, 'why are you reluctant to take up cricket in your schools?'. Miss Thomas, the head of Gateways Girls School, responded: 'Lack of accommodation is a big factor. We've no room for girls to play cricket. Also tennis is more useful socially and more the kind of accomplishment we like for our girls.'[69] One senses that the latter reason was the more important. There is evidence that some girls played in the face of opposition by their teachers; the Nottingham Girls' Grammar School Cricket Club wrote to *Women's Cricket* proudly proclaiming that they had formed in spite of 'adverse comment from the male population of our co-educational school', including the male staff.[70] Unfortunately this was not often possible.

Even those teachers who had permitted girls at their schools to play were not necessarily espousing progressive attitudes. Holland Park School, which was established in 1958 as one of the first ever comprehensive schools in England, was affiliated to the WCA by 1960. Holland Park's headmaster was asked why girls' cricket was not compulsory at his school but rather optional and played outside school hours. His response is worth reproducing almost in full:

> Tradition decrees that almost as soon as they can walk boys start playing cricket…. For girls there is no such compulsion…. They play in smaller groups than do boys and it is seldom that they are found playing team games…. When they take part in organised games at school the boys readily and naturally take to organised cricket…. For girls … organised games is often an introduction to team-playing…. A few of them may take to cricket … but they will be a small minority, a minority which will dwindle when faced with the hazards of the hard ball – and it is no good appealing to a girl's manliness if she declines to accept a chance of catching a full-blooded drive. Girls will not enjoy a game in which they have neither aptitude nor interest.[71]

---

[66]*Women's Cricket*, May 26, 1950.
[67]Ibid., August 28, 1959.
[68]Ibid., April 27, 1956.
[69]Ibid., September 5, 1958.
[70]Ibid., September 18, 1948.
[71]Ibid., August 12, 1960.

This is a good example of one of the trends noted by the PE Inspectorate, towards the underperformance of girls in PE lessons in mixed schools.[72] The Inspectorate felt that this was probably at least partly the result of teacher attitudes: 'headmistresses seem to have a better conception than headmasters of the function of P.E.... Head Masters tended to understand boys' needs better than girls.'[73] Clearly there were problems with ensuring that teachers, particularly male ones, accepted that all physical activities, including sports like cricket, could be shared by both boys and girls. Yet even the Inspectorate, as we have seen, agreed on the necessity of secondary-level girls following a separate programme from boys. The minutes of their meetings consistently support this point: typically, it was noted in 1953 that there was a difference between '[a] girl's subjective and aesthetic approach' to PE and 'a boy's need for objective achievement and his irritation with refinement and detail'.[74] This helped to justify the exclusion of cricket – as well as other sports, like football – from the schoolgirl's remit.

It does therefore appear that the main reasons why schoolgirl cricket was not introduced more widely into the new secondary modern and grammar schools were external to the WCA. The above comments show the affixed conservative attitudes to gender of those responsible for PE in schools at this time. It was these notions, and the consequent conclusion reached that cricket was not suitable or favourable as a school sport for girls, that prevented women's cricket from taking hold of the curricula of secondary modern and, later, comprehensive schools.

Conclusion

In the MCC's 1951 *Book for the Young Cricketer*, one of the winners of their essay competition 'Why I love Cricket' was a 17-year-old schoolgirl, Christine Maden. She wrote of the sport:

> Cricket is rich and virile, and has, even in restraint, a latent strength, which may leap excitingly at that moment when the game seems dullest.... In the flash of white flannels against the gleaming grass is the honesty, the justice, of cricket displayed, and, to me, the remembrance of it brings patience to await the spring.[75]

Schoolgirls who experienced it often felt the same passion for cricket as their male counterparts. It was, after all, England's national sport.

Yet the near-death of schoolgirl cricket by the 1970s meant that the experience of participating in the sport was denied to the majority of those who attended the new secondary modern and grammar schools. There are a variety of reasons for this. Lack of facilities certainly played its part, as many LEAs were reluctant to invest in the pitches and equipment necessary for school participation in cricket, preferring to focus on activities like swimming, netball and hockey. However, much of this reluctance was also due to the entrenched conservative attitudes of the educational authorities and some teachers, who continued to oppose female

---

[72] In fact this has remained an issue. See for example Oliver Leaman, *'Sit on the Sidelines and Watch the Boys Play': Sex Differentiation in Physical Education* (York: Schools Council, 1984).

[73] PE Inspectorate meeting, December 17 and 18, 1953, ED 158/115, TNA: PRO.

[74] Ibid.

[75] John St John, ed., *Book for the Young Cricketer*, 99.

participation in certain types of over-strenuous female activity, in this case cricket, after the Second World War. The best efforts of the WCA to engage with and reach out to the new secondary schools in the wake of the 1944 Education Act were therefore fruitless. As this case study has shown, in the years following the 1944 Act, the English education system remained not only divided along class lines, but along gender lines too. Indeed, the legacy of the decisions of those in authority in PE after the war is shown by the fact that PE in schools today remains gender-segregated, with very few girls able to participate in cricket.

Rebuilding physical education in the Western occupation zones of Germany, 1945–1949

Heather L. Dichter

Department of Sport Management and Media, Ithaca College, Ithaca, NY, USA

After the Second World War, the British, American and French believed education could be used to promote democracy in Germany. The Western powers faced particular difficulties with the field of physical education because of the strong Nazi influence in this area during the Third Reich. The premier pre-war physical education teacher training institute was located in the Soviet sector of Berlin. To help solve that problem as well as the dearth of qualified physical education teachers in post-war Germany, the Western Allies wanted to create a new institution for physical education. This article places the creation of the Deutsche Sporthochschule in Cologne within broader Allied education plans and goals for the occupation of Germany.

When the occupation of Germany began in 1945, the Allies were confronted with many difficulties in their efforts to transform Germany from a militaristic and Nazified country to a democratic society. The German education system largely ceased during the final year of the war, particularly in the large cities which faced frequent air raids and evacuations of children. The Allies knew that they needed to return the German educational system to a functional capability as soon as possible during the occupation. The Allies not only needed to rebuild the physical infrastructure for schools, they also needed to drastically change the curriculum so that it prepared the future generations of Germans to be democratic and willing participants in the international system. The previous 12 years of the Third Reich had completely disrupted the educational nature of the German school system in its ability to teach the youth of Germany the basics (and advanced components) of any subject within the curriculum.[1] The Western Allies believed German education could play an important role in their efforts to achieve their goals for Germany, especially demilitarisation and democratisation. Particularly troubling to the Allies was the extensive time spent on physical education in the Nazi schools and the militaristic activities contained therein. Within these broad plans for German education, the Western Allies also sought to create new institutions specifically for physical education

---

[1]James Tent, *Mission On the Rhine: Reeducation and Denazification in American-Occupied Germany* (Chicago: University of Chicago Press, 1982), 40–2; Ken Hardman, 'The Development of Physical Education in West Germany: General Background: from occupation to full sovereignty', *Physical Education Review* 4, no. 1 (1981): 48.

teacher training, which would promote democracy and fair play instead of militarism.

The impact of quadripartite division – of both Germany and Berlin – on physical education teacher training forced the Western Allies to address this educational problem separately from general education reform. The study of traditional university subjects and teacher training, courses which students could attend located across the country, prompted discussions of reform by each of the four occupation powers as well as Germans themselves. However, with the foremost pre-war physical education teaching training institute located in the Soviet sector of Berlin, the three Western Allies were forced to develop completely new institutions for this component of education. The result of British, American and French efforts to solve these problems and provide the theoretical and practical training for a new generation of physical education teachers was the creation of the Deutsche Sporthochschule, a college specifically devoted to the study of all aspects of physical education and sport.

As the divisions of the Cold War became more permanent, the three Western Allies – particularly the British and Americans – increasingly worked together in their efforts to rebuild Germany and enable the new German state to return to the international community. This article considers the creation of the Deutsche Sporthochschule within these broader actions of the three Western occupation powers. This postwar German sports university has previously been examined either within histories of the institution itself or else as part of biographies of its first rector, Carl Diem.[2] Wolfgang Buss and Franz Nitsch in particular attempt to de-emphasise Diem's role in the creation of the Deutsche Sporthochschule, arguing that much of the decision-making process fell to British and German education committees.[3] While Buss and Nitsch situate the creation of the institute within the aims of the British, who controlled the province (*Land*) in which Cologne lay, this approach nonetheless maintains the traditional and more narrow focus of examining education under only one occupation power in Germany. The ideas behind the creation of a new institute to train physical education teachers in the aftermath of the Second World War were not restricted to any one power or Germans residing solely in one occupation zone; thus, the plans to develop new physical education teacher training opportunities must be considered within the broader aims of the Western Allied powers and the actions they took in all three of their occupation zones. The creation of the Deutsche Sporthochschule was therefore neither a solely German nor British initiative but rather the practical solution that solved problems during the occupation which confronted all three western Allies and the Germans.

Sport in society

The general ideas behind sport for each of the four occupation powers as well as in Germany are important in understanding the attitudes which shaped Allied policies and actions during the occupation. The Western occupation powers understood the

---

[2] John G. Dixon, 'The Founding of the Cologne Sporthochschule', *Sports International* 6 (1982): 14–20; Frank Becker, *Den Sport gestalten: Carl Diems Leben (1882–1962)*, vol. 4 *Bundesrepublik* (Duisburg: Universitätsverlag Rhein-Ruhr, 2010), 35–80.

[3] Wolfgang Buss and Franz Nitsch, *Am Anfang war nicht Carl Diem – die Gründungsphase der Sporthochschule Köln 1945–1947* (Duderstadt: Mecke Druck und Verlag, 1986).

benefits of sport and physical education from their own domestic experiences. French politicians and nationalists had promoted physical exercise and sports clubs in the wake of the French surrender to the Germans at Sedan in 1870.[4] It was these concerns regarding the strength of the nation (or lack thereof) during the Third Republic which prompted Pierre de Coubertin to examine British and American physical education. This combination of French patriotism and the study of sport helped Coubertin develop the modern Olympic Games in the 1890s.[5]

In Britain and the United States, sport and education shared a strong tradition, including the belief that sport and physical education helped with character development in youth. Within Britain, the public schools – which produced a majority of the country's leaders – developed a strong emphasis on sport in the nineteenth century as a way to control rowdy and undisciplined pupils. Headmasters could monitor the free time of the students through games as well as impart their own ideals of what constituted a well-rounded or solid man of the British Empire.[6] The basis of sport in Great Britain – fair play, amateurism and health – also provided the grounding principles for the development of sport and physical education in North America. The large number and size of secondary schools and universities in the United States contributed to the adoption and regulation of sport within educational structures. This sport organisational structure reinforced meritocracy, a key ingredient of the American bourgeois ethos, which in turn helped maintain the democratic order.[7] The playground movement on both sides of the Atlantic also used sport as a method of social control and moral improvement for urban youth. Arising in concert with the idea of the settlement house as a response to the ills of inner-city slums at the end of the nineteenth century, the construction of playgrounds and supervised play-time for children helped alleviate social problems in American and British cities.[8]

American, British and French notions of sport differed from the ideas espoused by the fourth occupation power, the Soviet Union. What is often considered 'Soviet sport' – the state-run sport system which devoted significant resources and, at times, illegal drugs to the development of elite athletes – is in fact a postwar phenomenon. The Soviet Union withdrew from the modern Olympic movement following the Russian Revolution, only re-joining in time to participate in the 1952 Summer

---

[4]Richard Holt, *Sport and Society in Modern France* (Hamden, CT: Archon Books, 1981), 43–7.

[5]John J. MacAloon, *This Great Symbol: Pierre de Coubertin and the Origins of the Modern Olympic Games* (Chicago: University of Chicago Press, 1981).

[6]J.A. Mangan, *Athleticism in the Victorian and Edwardian Public School: The Emergence and Consolidation of an Educational Ideology*, 3rd ed. (London: Frank Cass, 1981; reprint, 2000), 34. Mangan's book in general traces the increased importance of athleticism within the public school system by looking at six schools in particular. Though specific headmasters emphasised athletics to a much higher degree than those at other schools, the nature of the public school system ensured the conformity of culture across the country.

[7]Andrei S. Markovits and Steven L. Hellerman, *Offside: Soccer & American Exceptionalism* (Princeton: Princeton University Press, 2001), 42–3.

[8]Allen Guttmann, *A Whole New Ball Game: An Interpretation of American Sports* (Chapel Hill: University of North Carolina Press, 1988), 83–5; Susan L. Tananbaum, 'Ironing Out the Ghetto Bend: Sports and the Making of British Jews', *Journal of Sport History* 31, no. 1 (2004): 53–7; David Dee, '"Nothing Specifically Jewish in Athletics"? Sport, Physical Recreation and the Jewish Youth Movement in London, 1895–1914', *London Journal* 34, no. 2 (2009): 81–100.

Olympic Games in Helsinki. Prior to the 1950s, however, Soviet or communist sport was vastly different from its postwar structure, attempting 'to advance revolutionary goals through political education directed at members of communist (and socialist) sport clubs'.[9] Furthermore, four straight years of directly fighting the German army left the Soviet Union quite familiar with the results of Nazi Germany's heavily emphasised physical education programme, which trained German boys to be soldiers. Both of these experiences therefore led the Soviets to view sport as being capable of serving political goals.

In addition to their own domestic sport histories, the four Allied powers' opinions regarding German sport and physical education influenced the policies they developed during the occupation. Physical education in Germany had expanded greatly during the Weimar Republic,[10] particularly with the establishment of the Deutsche Hochschule für Leibesübungen in 1920. One of Germany's prominent sports leaders, Carl Diem, was instrumental in the creation of this new institution responsible for promoting scientific research on sport as well as training physical education teachers. The Deutsche Hochschule für Leibesübungen was founded with great fanfare by the German president in the auditorium of Berlin's Friedrich-Wilhelm-Universität. The influential doctor, August Bier, served as the first rector with Carl Diem as the prorector. With the expansion of sport and physical education across the world throughout the 1920s and 1930s, the Deutsche Hochschule für Leibesübungen assumed a prominent and influential position and attracted visiting faculty from across Europe.[11] The Deutsche Hochschule für Leibesübungen, like other educational institutions and aspects of German life, was co-opted by the Nazis after 1933 through their policy of *Gleichschaltung* or coordination.[12] Sport during the Third Reich supported Nazi racial policies, particularly the creation of strong Aryans ready to serve the state as soldiers. To this end, the Nazis increased the time spent on physical education in the schools. The emphasis on physical training came directly from Hitler and was present from the early years of the Nazi Party. In *Mein Kampf* Hitler expounded on the importance of physical education over traditional academic education because the physically fit German 'is more valuable for the national community than a clever weakling'.[13] Young men in the Third Reich received at least two hours a day of physical training, sport and gymnastics in the regular school system, and the youth at the elite Adolf Hitler Schools spent five

---

[9]Barbara J. Keys, *Globalizing Sport: National Rivalry and International Community in the 1930s* (Cambridge, MA: Harvard University Press, 2006), 158–62; quote, 162.

[10]Roland Naul, 'History of Sport and Physical Education in Germany, 1800–1945', in *Sport and Physical Education in Germany*, ed. Roland Naul and Ken Hardman (London: Routledge, 2002), 22–4.

[11]Achim Laude and Wolfgang Bausch, *Der Sport-Führer: Die Legende um Carl Diem* (Göttingen: Verlag die Werkstatt, 2000), 40–1; Carl Diem, *Die Deutsche Hochschule für Leibesübungen* (Hannover: Continental-Caoutchouc-und Gutta-Percha-Compagnie, 1924). Laude and Bausch incorrectly state that Paul von Hindenburg was the German president present at the founding the Deutsche Hochschule für Leibesübungen, but Friedrich Ebert was president in 1920, which is seen in the photographs in Diem's work on the early years of the institute. Friedrich-Wilhelms-Universität is now the Humboldt University.

[12]G.A. Carr, 'The Synchronization of Sport and Physical Education Under National Socialism', *Canadian Journal of History of Sport and Physical Education* 10, no. 2 (1979): 20, 29; David Imhoof, 'Sharpshooting in Gottingen: A Case Study of Cultural Integration in Weimar and Nazi Germany', *German History* 23, no. 4 (2005): 460–93.

[13]Adolf Hitler, *Mein Kampf*, trans. Ralf Manheim (Boston: Houghton Mifflin, 1971), 408.

hours a day on physical education and only two hours a day on other subjects.[14] Hitler directly linked the physical training with the military, writing: 'To what extent the conviction of physical ability promotes a man's sense of courage, even arouses his spirit of attack, can best be judged by the example of the army.'[15] Physical education teachers, who had previously been marginalised within schools or released during the economic crisis of 1929, achieved a place of prominence within the schools during the Third Reich and often served as the deputy head teacher.[16] Physical education and sport were thus emphasised by the Nazis specifically to strengthen the nation and prepare for war. With this knowledge of sport during the Third Reich in addition to each of their own experiences with sport and physical education, the Allies not surprisingly addressed sport from the beginning of the occupation.

The occupation powers and education

Recognising the role that sport played in the remilitarisation of Germany, the Allies initially placed restrictions on sport via quadripartite Allied Control Authority Directive 23, which immediately addressed the punitive functions of the occupation.[17] The four powers also recognised that physical education tied sport to the reconstructive efforts of the military governments. The Western Allies in particular realised that sport and physical education, especially for the youth who had lived almost their entire lives under Nazi rule, could be utilised as a way to introduce democratic ideas to a wide segment of the German population. These Allied plans concerning physical education were therefore guided by the more general occupation policies regarding education.

Because education in the Third Reich had so extensively prepared German boys for military training, the Allies agreed in the summer of 1945 in the Potsdam Declaration that they would control education in Germany 'to eliminate Nazi and militarist doctrines and to make possible the successful development of democratic ideas'.[18] Education was therefore a necessary component 'to restore the stability of a peaceful German economy and to hold out hope for the ultimate recovery of

---

[14]Hitler, 409; Gerhard Rempel, *Hitler's Children: The Hitler Youth and the SS* (Chapel Hill: University of North Carolina Press, 1989), 177; Michael H. Kater, *Hitler Youth* (Cambridge, MA: Harvard University Press, 2004), 50.

[15]Hitler, 411.

[16]Arnd Krüger, 'Breeding, Rearing and Preparing the Aryan Body: Creating Supermen the Nazi Way', *International Journal of the History of Sport* 16, no. 2 (1999): 48.

[17]Heather L. Dichter, '"Strict measures must be taken": Wartime Planning and the Allied Control of Sport in Occupied Germany', *Stadion: International Journal of the History of Sport* 34, no. 2 (2008): 193–217.

[18]'Protocol of the Proceedings of the Berlin (Potsdam) Conference [Extracts],' in *Documents on Germany, 1944–1985* (Washington, DC: United States Department of State, 1985), 57. Technically only the United States, Great Britain and the Soviet Union signed the Potsdam Declaration. The French, who also received a zone of occupation, frequently used the argument that they had not agreed to the Potsdam Declaration when they disagreed with proposed quadripartite policies. On the whole, however, they supported the guiding principles found in the Potsdam Declaration. Tony Sharp, *The Wartime Alliance and the Zonal Division of Germany* (London: Oxford University Press, 1985).

national unity and self-respect'.[19] The restoration of the German education system entailed the denazification of the teaching profession, the demilitarisation of the curriculum and texts (including the heavy emphasis on physical training), the decentralisation of the system and the implementation of democratic ideals within the curriculum.

During the wartime planning for the occupation – before Allied troops entered Germany – the Allies had believed that youth would constitute a 'lost generation' because they had only ever lived under National Socialism. Once they began the occupation and spoke with Germans, the Allies noted 'that the Nazi system of indoctrination had been only partially successful'. Instead of finding the youth a lost generation, the Allies noted 'that particularly among the youngest a good share of the Nazi teachings were rejected'. The Americans noted that youth 'were tired of coercion and disillusioned by broken promises and false predictions'.[20] Once in Germany, Allied troops found more women and children than men or former soldiers, and the non-fraternisation ban initially imposed on troops quickly disappeared.[21] As the Allies increasingly worked with the Germans during the occupation, these interactions reinforced the weakness of Nazi ideas among German youth. This realisation prompted the Allies in 1946 to grant a general amnesty to all Germans born after 1 January 1919, except for those Germans classed as major offenders or offenders, categories which implied ardent support of the Nazi Party. This youth amnesty reflected the changed Allied opinion that Germans who had been 14 years old or younger when Hitler came to power in 1933 'had had little chance to know anything but Nazi ideology and they could not be excluded from society if they were to be rehabilitated'.[22] Rather than concentrate on denazification and demilitarisation, Allied education policies could focus on the promotion of democracy in school curricula and youth programmes.

---

[19]Long-Range Policy Statement for German Re-Education (SWNCC 269), May 16, 1946, Record Group [RG] 260, Records of the Education and Cultural Relations Division — Records of the Community Education Branch — Records of Mr E.L. Norrie, Branch Chief, Box 121, National Archives, College Park, Maryland (hereafter NA). Although this statement is from an American policy, it reflects the general Allied attitude regarding the role of education contained in the Potsdam Declaration.

[20]Letter, Konrad Kellen to Acting Chief of Intelligence, December 20, 1945, RG 260, Records of the Executive Office — The Office of Adjutant General: General Correspondence & otr recs (Decimal File). 1945–49, Box 87, NA; Kimberly A. Redding, *Growing Up in Hitler's Shadow: Remembering Youth in Postwar Berlin* (Westport, CT: Praeger, 2004). Kimberly Redding notes in several oral history testimonies in her examination of the Hitler Youth generation many of the reasons why German youth were not firm believers of Nazi ideas.

[21]Petra Goedde, *GIs and Germans: Culture, Gender, and Foreign Relations, 1945–1949* (New Haven: Yale University Press, 2003), 42–79.

[22]Lucius D. Clay, *Decision in Germany* (Garden City, NY: Doubleday & Company, 1950), 260; Dennis L. Bark and David R. Gress, *A History of West Germany*, 2nd ed., vol. 1, *From Shadow to Substance, 1945–1963* (Oxford: Basil Blackwell, 1993), 74–5; G.H. Garde to Directors, OMG-Bavaria, OMG-Greater Hesse, OMG-Wuerttemberg-Baden, OMG-Bremen Enclave, OMG-Berlin District, July 8, 1946, RG 260, Office of Military Government, Wuerttemberg-Baden — Records of the Education & Cultural Relations Div — Community Activ Branch Chief: Corresp & Rel Recs, 1945–49, Box 966, NA. The French did not implement the amnesty until May 2, 1947 with the promulgation of Ordonnance 92. 'Ordonnance No. 92 portant amnistie de la Jeunesse', *Journal Officiel du Commandement en Chef Français en Allemagne* (May 5, 1947): 700–1.

While the re-establishment of a political democracy in Germany was the goal of the Allies, they also understood that democracy was not something that could just be imposed on a country, as the problems of the Weimar Republic demonstrated to the creators of postwar policy. Germans needed to learn the values associated with ensuring a stable democracy, and education thus held an important position during the occupation. However, how to change education became a point of contention between the occupation powers and the Germans, particularly regarding the introduction of different educational features and systems. The four Allies ultimately agreed on basic principles for the democratisation of education with Allied Control Authority Directive No. 54, which they passed in 1947. This directive stated that 'all schools should lay emphasis upon education for civic responsibility and a democratic way of life, by means of the content of the curriculum, textbooks and materials of instruction, and by the organization of the school itself'. It also stipulated that 'all teacher education should take place in a university or in a pedagogical institution of university rank'.[23]

With this importance placed on education within the stated goals of the occupation, both the democratization and re-education of the Germans has long been of interest to scholars. One of the earliest works to focus solely on education during the occupation, James F. Tent's *Mission on the Rhine: Reeducation and Denazification in American-Occupied Germany* demonstrated the problems which 'hinder[ed] American efforts at "reeducating" the Germans toward democracy', particularly the American desire to create comprehensive secondary schools.[24] Because the Americans sought to completely reconfigure the German education system but were unable to achieve these changes, some scholars view American efforts as a failure.[25] More recently Karl-Heinz Fuessl and Gregory Paul Wegner have sought to refute this assessment, arguing that American youth policies outside the classroom 'achieved notable success' by introducing a 'new understanding of youth work and leisure'.[26] In contrast to American plans, the British were not intent on forcing educational reform based on set policies, instead seeking to interact as widely as possible with Germans involved in education in order to help the Germans 'create a new and healthy education in Germany'.[27] To the British, it was not the structure of the education system but rather the content that needed to be

---

[23]Allied Control Authority Control Council Directive No. 54, 3 July 1947, RG 260, Records of the Executive Office — The Office of Adjutant General: Allied Control Council Directives & Related Recs, 1945–49, Box 647, NA. James Tent states that this directive 'theoretically committed each member to produce common reforms. By most estimates the directive arrived two years too late.' Tent, 39.

[24]Tent, 12, 117.

[25]Jutta-B. Lange-Quassowski, *Neuordnung oder Restauration? Das Demokratiekonzept der amerikanischen Besatzungsmacht und die politische Sozialisation der Westdeutschen: Wirtschaftsordnung, Schulstruktur, Politische Bildung (Opladen: Leske Verlag, 1979).*

[26]Karl-Heinz Fuessl and Gregory Paul Wegner, 'Education under Radical Change: Education Policy and the Youth Program of the United States in Postwar Germany', *History of Education Quarterly* 36, no. 1 (1996): 1, 18.

[27]Robert Birley, *International Affairs* 26, no. 1 (Jan. 1950): 42; Raymond Ebsworth, *Restoring Democracy in Germany: The British Contribution* (London: Stevens & Sons, 1960); Arthur Heardnen, ed., *The British in Germany: Educational Reconstruction after 1945* (London: Hamish Hamilton, 1978). This desire to include Germans in the reconstruction of education in the British zone is reflected in many of the chapters in Hearnden's anthology that are written by former members of the Education Branch.

changed, and the British hoped to achieve a political re-education in Germany that would restore the 'principles of democratic thought and practice'.[28] The British viewed all levels of education as important, working equally on elementary and secondary schools, universities, and adult education.[29]

The French and Soviet occupation zones have generally received less attention than the American and British zones.[30] F. Roy Willis frames French policies regarding education as a successful step within the broader efforts to achieve a rapprochement between France and Germany.[31] Recent scholars have questioned whether French policies were as successful as Willis believed, although they do not refute the desire of the French to promote education and culture to overcome the long-standing Franco-German animosity.[32] Education in the Soviet zone, unlike in the three Western zones, underwent a dramatic transformation during the occupation as the Soviets sought to bring their zone of occupation into their sphere of influence through the implementation of communism. Benita Blessing has recently examined the 'new school', created during the occupation of the territory which became East Germany. In *The Antifascist Classroom: Denazification in Soviet-occupied Germany, 1945–1949*, Blessing demonstrates how this new communist education system shaped how the younger generation viewed themselves and Germany.[33] John Connelly has compared the Stalinisation of higher education in East Germany, Czechoslovakia and Poland, demonstrating the ways in which universities served 'as an instrument of ideological and social transformation'.[34] While Connelly expands the study of education in the Soviet zone and East Germany more broadly with other communist states in Eastern Europe, he nonetheless only addresses one of the four occupation powers.

---

[28]Arthur Hearden, 'The Education Branch of the Military Government of Germany and the Schools', in *The Political Re-Education of Germany and Her Allies After World War II*, ed. Nicholas Pronay and Keith Wilson (Totowa, NJ: Barnes & Noble Books, 1985), 100. David Welch noted that much of the literature on Britain's role in Germany 'was written during the height of the Cold War period [and] it was designed to present a particular ideological rationalization for Britain's occupying role and its re-education policy'. David Welch, 'The Political Re-Education of Germany after World War II: A Need for a Reappraisal?', *German History* 4 (Spring 1987): 24.

[29]Kurt Jürgensen, 'British Occupation Policy After 1945 and the Problem of "Re-education Germany"', *History* 68, no. 223 (1983): 230–1.

[30]In both countries the archival materials were closed longer than the American and British files.

[31]F. Roy Willis, *The French in Germany, 1945–1949* (Stanford: Stanford University Press, 1962), 247–8. Willis's book used published sources in the absence of French occupation material. Nonetheless, this text remains the standard English-language work on the French occupation.

[32]Richard Gilmore, *France's Postwar Cultural Policies and Activities in Germany: 1945–1956* (PhD diss., University of Geneva, 1971); Corine Defrance, *La politique culturelle de la France sur la rive gauche du Rhin 1945–1955* (Strasbourg: Presses Universitaires de Strasbourg, 1994); Monique Mombert, *Sous le signe de la rééducation: Jeunesse et Livre en Zone Française d'Occupation (1945–1949)* (Strasbourg: Presses Universitaires de Strasbourg, 1995); Stefan Zauner, *Erziehung und Kulturmission: Frankreichs Bildungs-Politik in Deutschland, 1945–1949* (Munich: R. Oldenbourg Verlag, 1994).

[33]Benita Blessing, *The Antifascist Classroom: Denazification in Soviet-occupied Germany, 1945–1949* (New York: Palgrave Macmillan, 2006), 5.

[34]John Connelly, *Captive University: The Sovietization of East German, Czech, and Polish Higher Education, 1945–1956* (Chapel Hill: University of North Carolina Press, 2000), 15.

These works considered education quite broadly, often focusing on zonal policies for the universities or secondary schools (or, in some cases, both); few works have attempted to consider education across zonal boundaries. The contributions in Manfred Heinemann's anthology on education policies in all four zones remain narrowly focused on specific *Länder* or zones rather than considering re-education across multiple zones.[35] Brian Puaca's recent work on education reform in West Germany does not follow the traditional periodisation of separating the occupation efforts from the German-run initiatives after the creation of the Federal Republic in 1949. However, Puaca examines the education structures in Hesse, which was fully part of the American zone, and West Berlin, which he considers a '"hot spot" in the pedagogical debates' during the Cold War.[36] Although addressing the impact of national policies at the local and regional level, Puaca's work still considers education largely as a legacy of just one occupation power.

Rather than take a comparative approach to physical education in all three of the Western zones, this article examines the combined efforts of the three Western Allies within the field of physical education teacher training. The Cold War was beginning to take shape in the late 1940s, and the Soviet blockade of Berlin in 1948–1949 demonstrated to the other three Allied powers the finality of the break with the Soviet Union regarding the ability to work together in Germany. The Berlin blockade in particular prompted the Western Allies to begin the process of amalgamating their three zones into the Federal Republic of Germany.[37] Thus, historical works on the occupation of Germany cannot continue to focus solely on actions in the American, British or French zones. Instead, scholars need to take into consideration the actions of all three powers because the Germans, alongside the Allied powers, had to work through the differences as the new German republic came into existence.

Rebuilding physical education

Although the Allies placed a heavy emphasis on education, they faced an immediate problem: the lack of qualified teachers in Germany in general, and particularly in the field of physical education. The foremost pre-war institution for physical education training in Germany, the Deutsche Hochschule für Leibesübungen, had been thoroughly Nazified during the Third Reich. In addition, noted the British, the best physical education instructors had received leading positions in the Hitler Youth (*Hitler Jugend*) or its affiliated League of German Girls (*Bund Deutscher Mädel*). Many of these instructors had been killed at the front or were now held as prisoners of war. Those instructors who were still in Germany were not allowed to re-enter the teaching profession because of their previous ties to the Nazi Party and its affiliated organisations. The dearth of suitable physical education teachers and the relationship between physical education and Nazi organisations forced the Allies to develop solutions to these problems in physical education. In addition to the

---

[35]Manfred Heinemann, ed., *Umerziehung und Wiederaufbau: die Bildungspolitik der Besatzungsmächte in Deutschland und Österreich* (Stuttgart: Klett-Cotta, 1981).

[36]Brian M. Puaca, *Learning Democracy: Education Reform in West Germany, 1945–1965* (New York: Berghahn Books, 2009), 6.

[37]Lucius D. Clay, *Decision in Germany* (Garden City, NY: Doubleday, 1950), 212; Carolyn Eisenberg, *Drawing the Line: The American Decision to Divide Germany, 1944–1949* (Cambridge: Cambridge University Press, 1996), 411–93.

LIVERPOOL JOHN MOORES UNIVERSITY
LEARNING SERVICES

problem of too few qualified physical education teachers, the Allies also had to address the issue of where physical education teachers could be trained. The Deutsche Hochschule für Leibesübungen now lay in the Soviet sector of the divided capital. Other physical education teacher training programmes had existed at universities across Germany, including in the Western zones of occupation, but these faculties had also been forced to adopt Nazi policies during the Third Reich. Activities could not resume until these institutions and their faculties underwent the formal denazification process and received approval by their zonal occupation power for the universities to reopen. These complications in resuming physical education teacher training were on top of the difficulties in securing classroom space for university courses in the aftermath of the war. Few universities and *Hochschulen* had even 50% of their buildings and facilities; those lucky institutions with less damage often had to accommodate Allied troops or were requisitioned for other uses.[38] This combination of circumstances left the field of physical education – both in schools and in the training of the teachers – in need of significant Allied assistance.

The large role that Americans believed sport could play in the education of Germans was evident by its inclusion in the report completed by the 1946 Education Mission to Germany, often called the Zook Report after its chairman, George F. Zook.[39] Although the Zook Report did not specifically refer to physical education teacher training, its recommendations addressed the training of teachers and youth leaders (including for sport). Teacher training, the report noted, should seek to teach 'the free interchange of opinion, orderly debate, and other devices and techniques which will enable boys and girls under their care to understand democracy and to live in its spirit'.[40] The Zook Report's section on youth activities noted that approximately one-quarter of the two million German youth in the American zone participated in extra-curricular activities, with nearly 40% engaged in sport.[41] Physical education and sports activities, the report recommended, should emphasise 'health, hygiene, and recreational features', and military government should develop programmes to train leaders for youth activities so that they could foster 'democratic ways of thinking and living'.[42] Taken together, the Americans' general

---

[38]David Phillips, 'The Re-opening of Universities in the British Zone: The Problem of Nationalism and Student Admissions', in *German Universities after the Surrender: British Occupation Policy and the Control of Higher Education*, ed. David Phillips (Oxford: University of Oxford Department of Educational Studies, 1983), 4; *Report of the United States Education Mission to Germany* (Washington, DC: United States Government Printing Office, 1946), 7. This report noted nearly 350 elementary schools in the American zone alone were serving in capacities other than for education.

[39]Fred W. Buddy, 'George Frederick Zook: An Analysis of Selected Contributions of an American Educator' (PhD diss., University of Akron, 1990), 41–6. Zook had been a history professor, a university president, and, since 1934, president of the American Council on Education. Zook had first worked for the government during the First World War by serving on the Committee on Public Information.

[40]*Report of the United States Education Mission*, 25.

[41]The British as well noted the high participation of youth in sports clubs over other types of cultural or religious clubs. Report on Youth Movement Activities During Month of February 1946, March 7, 1946, Foreign Office (FO) 1050/13, National Archives of the United Kingdom, Kew, Richmond, Surrey (hereafter UKNA).

[42]*Report of the United States Education Mission*, 34. The youth activities section was written by Paul M. Limbert, a YMCA official who assumed the presidency of Springfield College in Massachusetts upon his return from Germany. Paul M. Limbert, *Reliving a Century* (Asheville, NC: Biltmore Press, 1997), 140–1.

concern regarding teacher training and the role of sport within youth activities thus demonstrated a commitment to physical education teacher training even though no policy specifically addressed that group of educators.

The following year the athletic directors from the University of Colorado and Rutgers University spent 60 days touring the American zone to make recommendations regarding physical education and sport. They noted that 'every reasonable effort should be made to facilitate the training of physical education teachers' because 'very few able physical education leaders' existed in Germany. One of their main recommendations was that 'intensive attention should be given to the German physical education Teacher Training schools'. They also noted the difficulty of many schools in hiring full-time physical education instructors, and they therefore suggested providing 'special lectures' for current teachers so that they could also qualify to supervise physical education activities.[43] These two visiting experts, sponsored by the American Military Government, were not the only people to note these problems and suggest the need for more physical education teacher training.

The French sought to resume education in Germany as quickly as possible after the war, but they struggled in their efforts to promote physical education. The French Military Government was actually the first of the Allies to reopen a German university when they re-established the University of Mainz, which had previously been open from 1477 to 1817. Although it had not existed for over 100 years, the fact that a university had previously existed in the city, plus the available air force barracks to accommodate students, enabled the French to re-found the University of Mainz.[44] The French also wanted to create an institute to train physical education instructors and began studying this possibility in July 1946. The French had already reduced physical education in the schools in their zone to two or three hours a week.[45] Although they preferred a set course of instruction for the schools, the small number of qualified instructors and lack of sufficient equipment initially prevented more standardisation. To alleviate these problems, the French wanted to develop university courses for physical education teachers.

The French first attempted to establish an institute for physical education instruction at the University of Mainz and, over the next few months, considered similar programmes at Trier, Tübingen and Tailfingen. In each city the French authorities ran into practical and material difficulties in opening a school for physical education instructors. The biggest problem confronting the French Military Government in implementing physical education programmes was the lack of instructors. None of these French efforts to create a physical education institute

---

[43]Henry G. Carlson and George E. Little to Chief, Education and Religious Affairs Branch, Report on Physical Education, n.d. [1947], Folder 6, Box 178, Series I, Central Administration President's Office, University of Colorado at Boulder Archives, Boulder, Colorado.

[44]F. Roy Willis, *The French in Germany, 1945–1949* (Stanford: Stanford University Press, 1962), 174–5, 247–48; Richard Gilmore, *France's Postwar Cultural Policies and Activities in Germany: 1945–1956* (PhD diss., University of Geneva, 1971), 119–21.

[45]Rapport, de Monsieur le Lieutenant de Vaisseau De Mesnil-Adelee to de Monsieur le Lt-Colonel de Champvallier, July 19, 1946, Affaires Culturelles (AC) 416/3, Bureau des archives de l'Occupation française en Allemagne et en Autriche, Colmar (hereafter AOFAA).

therefore came to fruition.[46] Even the physical education training school that was to be established in the semi-detached Saar to 'teach the French methods of sport' was delayed because of bad weather, the poor state of the facilities, and a lack of material and equipment.[47]

At the end of the year the French again considered the creation of physical education and sports centres in their zone. Dr Otto Peltzer, a former world record-holding runner in the 1920s whom the Nazis had imprisoned, had recently arrived in the French zone and proposed the creation of a sports college (*Sportakademie*) in Rhineland-Pfalz. Peltzer argued that a new generation of sports instructors needed to be developed 'as soon as possible' because most of the physical education teachers in German schools had 'received a militarist and nationalist training' and should be removed.[48] The French Military Government agreed that this sports college or a physical education centre created along similar lines would be desirable. They believed that the establishment of such a school could begin in the spring of 1947 if the location of physical premises and instructors did not run into too many problems.[49]

At the same time that the French attempted to create a physical education teacher training school in their zone and the Americans considered the recommendations of the Zook Report and the visiting athletic directors, the British also sought to establish a physical education college in their zone. They too recognised the severe shortage of qualified physical education instructors. The British believed that 'the present generation of German children should not be denied a liberal physical education because the minds, as well as the bodies of their fathers, were used to further ignoble ends'.[50] The British Military Government's Education Advisory Committee noted in 1946 the 'serious shortage' of sports instructors in Germany and agreed to create a training programme as soon as possible. Noting that the German-run Zonal Sport Committee (*Zonensportrat*) in the British zone had suggested creating an interzonal sports university, the British began making preparations. Unlike the French, the British were able to locate the resources to establish a physical education college in their zone. Because the pre-war physical education academy in Berlin had trained teachers for all of Germany, their new physical

---

[46]Situation Statistique, Secrétariat Général, Division Education Publique, May 1, 1947, AC 415/2, AOFAA; Rapport, de Monsieur le Leiutenant de Vaisseau De Mesnil-Adelee to de Monsieur le Lt-Colonel de Champvallier, July 19, 1946, AC 416/3, AOFAA; Situation Statistique, Secrétariat Général, Division Education Publique, August 1, 1947, AC 415/2, AOFAA; Situation Statistique, Secrétariat Général, Division Education Publique, November 1, 1947, AC 415/2, AOFAA; Documentation générale concernant l'œuvre accomplie en ZFO de 1945 à 1949 par la Division Education Publique, n.d., AC 845/1, AOFAA.

[47]Rapport, de Monsieur le Lieutenant de Vaisseau De Mesnil-Adelee to de Monsieur le Lt-Colonel de Champvallier, July 19, 1946, AC 416/3, AOFAA; Situation Statistique, Secrétariat Général, Division Education Publique, May 1, 1947, AC 415/2, AOFAA. France had hoped to gain Saarland as territory for itself after the war. Although Saarland competed with its own Olympic team in 1956 – separate from both France and Germany – the people of the Saar had already voted to rejoin the Federal Republic of Germany. Wolfgang Harres, *Sportpolitik an der Saar, 1945–1957* (Saarbrücken: Saarbrücker Dr. und Verl., 1997).

[48]December 1946 Rapport Mensuel, Rhénanie-Hesse-Nassau, Jeunesse et Sport, January 3, 1947, Rhenanie-Palatinat (RP) 446/2, AOFAA.

[49]December 1946 Rapport Mensuel, Rhénanie-Hesse-Nassau, Jeunesse et Sport, January 3, 1947, RP 446/2, AOFAA.

[50]J.G. Dixon, HMI's Report on Physical Education in Germany, October 1948, FO 1050/1255, UKNA.

Figure 1.   Chief Sports Officer J.G. Dixon.

education school would not be restricted only to Germans residing in the British zone. To that end, the British agreed that this new school would be a joint venture with the Americans.[51]

The Zonal Education Advisory Committee discussed possible sites for this new sports university. When Brunswick was suggested as a possibility, the representative from Hanover argued that the new sports college must be in a university town so that the students would also have the opportunity for academic study of subjects other than sport. The committee then considered Frankfurt (in the American zone) and Cologne (in the British zone). The British pointed out that American forces occupied the Frankfurt site and would be unlikely to relinquish it. They therefore went ahead to secure the Cologne site to begin planning immediately.[52] The Chief Sports Officer for the British zone, J.G. Dixon (Figure 1), had also preferred Cologne for 'the beauty of its woodland setting' and, naturally, because it would be easier for him to monitor if the sports university were in the British zone.[53]

Following several levels of screening and discussions with their Chief Sports Officer, the British offered the position of rector of the new sports university to Carl

[51]Minutes, Third meeting, Zonal Education Advisory Committee, August 26, 1946, FO 1005/1576, UKNA.

[52]Minutes, Fourth meeting, Zonal Education Advisory Committee, October 3, 1946, FO 1005/1576, UKNA.

[53]John G. Dixon, 'The Founding of the Cologne Sporthochschule', *Sports International* 6 (1982): 16–17.

Diem. Diem had been a member of the Organising Committee for the 1936 Olympic Games in Berlin, which the International Olympic Committee awarded to Germany before Hitler rose to power. Diem had succeeded Bier as rector of the Deutsche Hochschule für Leibesübungen until the Nazis relieved him of his duties. Diem had lost that position, along with a lectureship at the Friedrich-Wilhelm-Universität in Berlin, because he was too heavily involved in the Weimar system and its 'Jewish environment', whereas the Nazis placed importance on what they considered 'German' and 'Aryan' physical education.[54] Although Diem was nearly 65 years old when hired as rector of the sports university, Dixon selected Diem because 'the youth were inexperienced and the middle-aged often tainted. Only among the old could one find proven eminence combined with detachment from Nazism.'[55] Of course, Diem's background was not so neatly anti-Nazi, as evidenced two years later by the renewed investigations into his past activities when the Germans re-founded their Olympic committee and applied to re-join the International Olympic Committee.[56] While this article does not attempt to dismiss this debate, what is important with regard to the founding of the Deutsche Sporthochschule is what the Allies believed and said in 1946–1947 in order to proceed with the appointment of Diem as the first rector for the new sports university.

After meeting with Dixon, Diem wrote an essay about the principles on which the instruction at the new physical education college should be based, which coincided with the idea that the occupation powers held regarding sport. From the beginning, Diem stated that 'sport in Germany must again serve the ideals of health, fair-play, democracy, culture and international friendship'. He continued that 'the Nazi emphasis upon a militaristic and muscle-building gymnastics' should be replaced. 'Instead of the Nazi mass-drill and striving after "uniformity", Physical Education must concern itself fundamentally with the individual, and must lead him to harmony.'[57] Diem thus saw physical education coinciding with the aims of the Allies, both to remove the effects of Nazi control of the discipline and to help

---

[54]J.G. Dixon to Director of Education and Col. Walker, December 9, 1947, FO 1013/2213, UKNA; S.M. Armetage and W.J. Bracey-Gibbon, Cologne Intelligence Section, Vetting of University Professors: Dr. Karl Keim [sic], July 21, 1947, FO 1050/1188, UKNA; Carl Diem, 'Bericht über meine Tätigkeit während der Zeit des Nationalsozialismus', June 16, 1946, Diem, Carl – Physical Educ. College, 1946–1947, Box 10, R.T. Alexander Papers, University of Virginia Library, Charlottesville, Virginia.

[55]Dixon, 17.

[56]Carl Diem's life, and particularly the question of to what extent his own beliefs aligned with National Socialism and the ideas promoted during the Third Reich, has been a frequent topic of debate, both at the time and more recently. For the Allied discussions in the late 1940s and early 1950s regarding Diem's activities, see Chapter 5 in Heather L. Dichter, *Sporting Democracy: The Western Allies' Reconstruction of Germany Through Sport, 1944–1952* (PhD diss., University of Toronto, 2008). For the more recent debate in Germany, see Ralf Schäfer, 'Sportgeschichte und Erinnerungspolitik: Der Fall Carl Diem', *Zeitschrift für Geschichtswissenschaft* 58, no. 11 (2010): 877–99; Michael Krüger, 'Zur Debatte um Carl Diem', *Zeitschrift für Geschichtswissenschaft* 59, no. 3 (2011): 201–9; Hubert Dwertmann, 'Die Beteiligung von Sportfunktionäen im NS-Regime und ihr Einfluss auf die Sportgeschichtsschreibung nach 1945', *Zeitschrift für Geschichtswissenschaft* 59, no. 3 (2011): 230–41; Frank Becker, 'Carl Diem und der Nationalsozialismus', *Zeitschrift für Geschichtswissenschaft* 59, no. 3 (2011): 242–51.

[57]Carl Diem, Principles upon which instruction at the Bi-Zonal Physical Education College at Cologne should be based, March 25, 1947, Mappe 212, Carl und Liselott Diem Archiv, Deutsche Sporthochschule, Cologne (hereafter CULDA).

create a positive image of Germans. In addition, the creation of the Sporthochschule would address the numerical problem of available teachers. Diem stated that not only were formal teachers needed, but also amateur sports instructors because 'a higher proportion of these teachers and instructors than of other professional men was both forced into the Party and killed in the war (for similar reasons). The need for new teachers is therefore greater than it ever has been before.'[58]

Thus, the Deutsche Sporthochschule (or, as the British called it, the Bi-Zonal Physical Education College of Cologne University) opened in the summer of 1947, with Diem leading a staff of nine (six men and three women). A similar gender ratio existed among the students, with 35 women among the 100 students enrolled during the first semester.[59] Students came primarily from the British zone (85), although students from the other three zones all attended from the outset. Even though the facilities (Figures 2 and 3), both for sport and for living, were not complete when classes began that summer, the competence and enthusiasm of Diem's staff contributed to Dixon's high opinion of the efforts of the Sporthochschule.[60] The third semester saw an increase in percentage of pupils from the American zone, although students from the British zone still comprised the highest number.[61]

The majority of the students who enrolled at the Deutsche Sporthochschule were born after 1 January 1919 and thus fell under the general youth amnesty. Nonetheless, a denazification committee still reviewed every student's application and background because of the high level of nazification of physical education and sport. The majority of the students began their studies having passed the *Abitur*, the German school-leaving exam that enabled students to attend university. The Sporthochschule permitted some students who had not passed or taken the *Abitur* to study as *Gasthörer*, students on a one-year probationary period. This process provided an opportunity for students who 'showed high ability even if they lacked the academic qualification'.[62] The nature of education under the Nazis, combined with the difficulties of actually carrying out education during the latter stages of the war and the beginning of the occupation, from the lack of both teachers and infrastructure, left many men and women without the necessary university qualifications. By providing this additional opportunity for students who lacked the *Abitur*, the Western Allies demonstrated a commitment to expanding physical education teacher training in Germany.

---

[58] Carl Diem, Principles upon which instruction at the Bi-Zonal Physical Education College at Cologne should be based, March 25, 1947, Mappe 212, CULDA.

[59] Women far outnumbered men during the occupation period as a result of the many wartime deaths and the prisoners of war still in captivity. In addition, the number of 14- to 18-year-old males in Berlin, for example, plummeted from 108,000 in 1939 to approximately 26,000 in 1945. The Zook Report noted in 1946 that the disproportionate ratio of men to women in Germany, combined with the need for young widows to earn a living, prompted many women in their early twenties to find it 'necessary or desirable to enter the teaching profession'. Redding, 46; *Report of the United States Education Mission*, 26.

[60] Monthly Report for July 1947, E/RA, HQ MG, Regierungsbezirk Cologne, July 25, 1947, FO 1013/2201, UKNA.

[61] Of a total of 280 students enrolled in the third term, 218 were from the British zone, 33 from the American zone, 16 from the French zone, and 10 from the Soviet zone. Another three students were non-Germans (one Greek, one Yugoslav, and one Hungarian). J.G. Dixon, Report on the Physical Education College of Cologne University, Summer Term 1948, June 18, 1948 (received), FO 1050/1188, UKNA.

[62] J.G. Dixon to Mr. Birley, December 15, 1947 (received), FO 1050/1188, UKNA.

Figure 2.   The Deutsche Sporthochschule from the year it opened (1947). The pictures are from an album created by J.G. Dixon and held in possession of his son, John Dixon.

The French, who had made some of the earliest attempts to develop a physical education school in their zone, were ultimately unable to locate the financial and physical resources to create their own institution. While they hinted to the Americans in May 1948 that they were still thinking of creating their own physical education school in their zone, these comments were largely a way to secure more places at the Sporthochschule for Germans from the French zone.[63] By the end of 1948, a year after the sports university opened in Cologne, the French Military Government believed that a separate sports university in their zone would create a lack of uniformity in training that would, in the long run, create serious difficulties for physical education in Germany.[64] By this time, the three Western zones had begun the process of amalgamation that resulted in the creation of the Federal Republic the following year. The Western Allies began taking steps to transfer control to the Germans, including in the field of education.[65] The Western Allies and Germans had therefore recognised the advantage of having one premier sports university for what would soon become one state.

While the primary aim of the sports university was to provide full university training in all aspects of physical education and its related scientific fields, it also provided shorter courses and certificates for teachers already in the schools who were not trained in physical education (Figure 4). The creation of the sports university therefore addressed the basic problem of a small number of available teachers. For the beginning of the third term, the sports university instituted a one-year

---

[63]Memorandum, Conversation with Mr Dumesnil, the Chief of Physical Education and Sports, French Zone, May 3, 1948, RG 260, Records of the Education and Cultural Relations Division – Records of the Community Education Branch – Records re the Work of the Youth Activities Section, Box 150, NA. The Chief of Physical Education and Sports for the French Zone, after complaining about the lack of places for students from the French Zone and stating the desire to open an institute in the French zone, then agreed to visit the Sporthochschule 'before taking any further steps'.

[64]1948 Compte-rendu d'activité du Bureau de l'Education physiques et des sports en ZFOA, November 25, 1948, AC 415/1, AOFAA.

[65]Tent, 307–10.

Figure 3. The Deutsche Sporthochschule from the year it opened (1947). The pictures are from an album created by J.G. Dixon and held in possession of his son, John Dixon.

post-certificate course for elementary school teachers in which six women and eight men enrolled. The teachers, seconded from their school for the year, learned how they could provide instruction in physical education in 'badly equipped Volksschulen as well as in the very few which still possess a gymnasium in working order'.[66] These programmes were exactly what the two American university athletic directors had recommended during their 1947 visit.

The Sporthochschule also hosted brief courses with experts from abroad which were part of larger Allied efforts to foster democracy in Germany. All three Western powers established numerous programmes that brought experts to Germany for up to 90 days to help further the reconstruction and democratisation of Germany.[67] A two-week course over Easter 1949 brought six physical education teachers from British secondary schools to the Sporthochschule to provide lectures and practical

---

[66]Monthly Report (Education) for February 1949, Regierungsbezirk Cologne, February 22, 1949, FO 1013/2205, UKNA; J.G. Dixon, Report on the Physical Education College of 42 Cologne University, Summer Term 1948, June 18, 1948 (received), FO 1050/1188, UKNA.

[67]Henry J. Kellermann, *Cultural Relations as an Instrument of U.S. Foreign Policy: The Educational Exchange Program Between the United States and Germany, 1945–1954* (Washington, DC: Government Printing Office, 1978); Education Summary No. 72 Berlin, K.J.W. Melvin for Educational Adviser, April 16, 1947, FO 1050/1256, UKNA; Dixon, 19. The British also sent two physical education specialists to spend a week in each of the four provinces of the British zone in 1947, followed by visits from two female physical education specialists.

Figure 4. Elementary school teachers invited to study physical education at the Deutsche Sporthochschule. Photographs from an album created by J.G. Dixon and held in possession of his son, John Dixon.

work for 25 male and 25 female German physical education teachers.[68] Another two-week course in August 1949 for 20 physical education teachers from North Rhine-Westphalia and five from Berlin was held at the Sporthochschule and led by the coordinator of physical education for London County Council and assisted by two British secondary school teachers.[69] The British sought to foster closer ties between educators from both countries, which they believed would have a long-lasting impact.[70]

Conclusion

In reporting on the first semester of the Deutsche Sporthochschule's existence, British Chief Sports Officer J.G. Dixon noted that a disagreement over dormitory regulations had arisen between faculty and students. The problem presented an

---

[68]Monthly Report, December 1948, Education Branch, January 4, 1949, FO 1050/1103, UKNA.

[69]Points Arising from the Twenty-Sixth Conference of CEOs, Bad Rothenfelde, April 28–29, 1949, FO 1050/1112, UKNA.

[70]Dixon, 19. Following a two-week visit in 1948 by the Head of the Physical Education Department of Birmingham University, the two institutions established a long-running faculty and student exchange.

opportunity for the newly created student government to demonstrate the positive influence of self-government in achieving a resolution. Dixon noted that this type of experience 'of a self-regulated community life is the most valuable part of their education' and that 'the shaping of the theory by practical experience is of first-rate importance'.[71] Diem, too, noted that 'sport teachers must educate youth to democracy, and develop its faculties of self-government, for sport is based upon free-will, friendship, and fair-play, and the solution of the self-governmental tasks implied thereby corresponds to the urges of youth'.[72] This desire for a student-run component coincided with other initiatives introduced in Germany at the time. The ability of youth to participate in democratic institutions provided a much greater learning opportunity through actual experience rather than merely learning about democracy in a classroom.[73]

Unlike much of the literature on education during the occupation of Germany, which often criticises the lack of success regarding educational reform by the various Allied powers, the creation of the Deutsche Sporthochschule provides an example which the Western powers perceived as a success. As the Chief Sports Officer for the British zone, J.G. Dixon had emphasised 'the desperate need for new, young and well-trained physical training instructors in schools in the Zone'.[74] Establishing a school specifically for physical education and the training of physical education teachers provided a practical solution to the problem of a lack of qualified physical education teachers, which all three Western powers sought to alleviate. In addition, the creation of the Deutsche Sporthochschule aimed 'to break down the traditional rigid separation of sports and academic subjects in German education'.[75] Students studied various sports, dance, movement, children's games, anatomy, physiology and health as part of their teacher training preparations.[76] Furthermore, the placement of the Deutsche Sporthochschule in Cologne, a city with a university that the sports students could also attend, coincided with one of the recommendations of the Zook Report. The Americans on the Education Mission noted the importance of the training provided by pedagogic institutes, but they also advocated that universities take a greater role in the training of elementary and secondary teachers.[77]

During the occupation of Germany, quadripartite (and later tripartite) agreements established general policies for which each occupation power then created its own programmes to meet those goals. Attempts to reform German education happened separately in each zone. British and American cooperation, and the support of the

---

[71]J.G. Dixon, Report on Bi-Zonal Physical Education College of Cologne University, December 1947–January 1948, February 16, 1948 (received), FO 1050/1188, UKNA.

[72]Carl Diem, Principles upon which instruction at the Bi-Zonal Physical Education College at Cologne should be based, March 25, 1947, Mappe 212, CULDA.

[73]Brian M. Puaca, '"We Learned What Democracy Really Meant": The Berlin Student Parliament and Postwar School Reform in the 1950s', *History of Education Quarterly* 45, no. 4 (2005): 616.

[74]Minutes, 18th Conference of Senior Education Control Officers, May 5–6, 1947, FO 1050/1255, UKNA.

[75]Minutes, Fifth Conference of Youth Control Officers, Hannover, November 18, 1947, FO 1050/1174, UKNA.

[76]Report by Mr Munrow, Head of Birmingham University Dept. of Physical Education, n.d. [August 1948], FO 1023/2213, UKNA. Although Munrow, after a two-week visit, felt that the Sporthochschule 'falls short as a University course', he nonetheless felt that it 'has great potentialities as a course for Physical Education'.

[77]*Report of the United States Education Mission*, 26–7.

French, on the creation of the Deutsche Sporthochschule provides an early example of Western Allied cooperation outside of the Allied Control Authority. Although the British were the dominant power in fostering the establishment of a college for physical education and maintained a significant interest in its running because of its location in the British zone, the Deutsche Sporthochschule nonetheless served the needs of the Americans and French.

The Allies wanted to utilise education to instil democratic values in pupils particularly because of the Nazi misuse of the education system and authoritarian control of German life. Although the Allies sought to remove militarised sport from the German curriculum, they did not want to remove sport completely from German education. The Americans and British in particular believed in the importance of physical education, as evidenced by the emphasis of sport within their own domestic educational curricula. The military governments needed teachers who were not fully indoctrinated in Nazi ideology or methods, a potentially difficult requirement to fulfil in the immediate post-war period because of the heavy emphasis placed on physical training during the Third Reich. The division of Germany forced the Western Allies to create a new institution to help relieve the primary problem of a lack of qualified non-Nazi German personnel to provide sport instruction with a democratic emphasis. The Allies hoped that a new generation of Germans would mature with a solid foundation of democratic principles, particularly through their participation in physical education without militarism.

Acknowledgements

The author would like to thank Sarah Teetzel and the anonymous reviewers for their helpful comments, and Luke Harris for his assistance with obtaining the photographs. John Dixon kindly granted me access to his father's materials, as well as permission to include the photographs here.

Images of the body: the Greek physical education curriculum since the Second World War

Dimitris Foteinos

Faculty of Philosophy-Pedagogy-Psychology, University of Athens, Athens, Greece

Between the years 1950 and 1974 there was a conservative view regarding physical education (PE) and the perception of the body in Greek PE curricula. PE was seen as an ideological means of legitimising political dominance. Before the Athens Olympic games of 2004, educational authorities were assigned the duty of promoting the Olympic spirit in education, and a new PE and sports curriculum was developed. The main question of this paper is why PE was not perceived as an autonomous subject, but had to be related to the State's major political and ideological agendas, in the context of both dictatorship and democracy. A Foucauldian perspective is adopted concerning perceptions of the body as an agent of power, and Bernstein's framework will be used to analyse PE curricula.

Stretching the historical background: the ancient Greek world and the political body

It was known in ancient times (*νοῦς ὑγιὴς ἐν σώματι ὑγιε – mens sana in corpore sano – a healthy/sound mind in a healthy/sound body*) that mental enhancement should be accompanied by a healthy body.[1] In other words, a healthy mind presupposes a healthy body – or, alternatively, a healthy mind is the precondition for a healthy body. In any case, in the ancient – both Greek and Roman – world, body and mind were thought of as a unique condition of existence, a holistic perspective of the human condition.

Healthiness, the social condition for health promotion, was perceived under the perspectives of *Keadas*, on one side (the Spartan tradition of healthiness and physical strength), and of the *political body*, on the other: in the Athenian political sphere, the 'body' was part of the treasury of the *polis* and the guardian of its

---

[1] The origin of the Latin phrase is the poet Juvenal: in his poem Satire X, he tried to answer the question as to what people should desire, and pray for, in life. The Greek phrase comes from the sixth century BC, and was used during the Olympic Games. Since then it has become a motto for the interconnection and relationship between the state of the body and the state of the mind, and in particular the balance between them.

vitality and prosperity. Individual citizens of the Athenian *polis* conceded some of their *ad rem* inherent rights to the *polis*, in return for certain political rights, such as the right to elect and be elected to public offices, and the right to a high standard of living through the activities of the *polis*.[2]

A 'mind' incorporated into such a body must be able to control the body's sluggishness and idleness. Healthiness of mind, perceived as such, became the benchmark for democracy: democracy could be earned only by citizens obtaining the free will and the conscience to deliberately transfer certain of their individual rights to an institutional formation that was larger than any individual could manipulate.[3] Political identity, as an individual right, was claimed through democracy. Therefore, the well-built, healthy and strong body that was accompanied by a strong political mentality was democratically engaged, and guaranteed the well-being, prosperity and persistence of the *polis*.

In accordance with this perception of the body and its relation to the mind, physical activity was part of the daily routine of childhood and adolescence (among free-born males), where the body, especially the well-formed, healthy and strong body, and the well-educated mind were viewed as the outcome of a good upbringing. This 'whole', the well-formed and well-built body fitted with an educated mind, was the ultimate guardian of civic life and prosperity. In the gymnasium, young people and elders were communicating, interacting and strengthening the spirit of democracy and of the *polis*.[4] So, as far as physical activity is concerned, there was a strong philosophical and political tradition interwoven with democracy itself, at least during the period of classic Athenian democracy.[5]

Nevertheless, physical activity was praised throughout ancient Greece, resulting in, among other things, the establishment of the Olympic Games (and other major games as well), as a means to expand peace among *poleis*. In this perspective, the Olympic Games played both a political and an educational role – the promotion of unity among Greeks, based on shared cultures – as each athlete was representing himself alone, without any territorial affiliation, while the games were accompanied by religious ceremonies and theatrical presentations.[6] It could be argued that the athletes in the Olympic Games were the epitome of ancient Greek model citizens: they were in the best physical condition, mentally capable of comprehending and discussing philosophical and political issues, skilled in music or other arts, and, finally, socially equipped to take part in all the activities of the *polis* while conceding some of their individual rights to it. Physical activities and education, then, in the ancient Greek period, were not separate from 'political' or citizenship education,

---

[2]Thucydides, *History of the Peloponnesian War* (trans. by Koutalopoulos, Athens: Pataki Editions, 2012), 2.41.1: 'and therefore, we claim the whole of the polis as school for Greece, since our polis throughout its activities stands as a model'.

[3]Thucydides 2.38.1–2, and 2.39.4.

[4]Daniel McLean and Amy Hurd, *Kraus' Recreation and Leisure in Modern Society* (Ontario: Jones and Bartlett Publishers, 2012), 53.

[5]Plato, *Republic* (Athens: Kaktos Publications, 1992), 376 a–c, 403 d–e, 412 a. Plato in his *Republic* declared that physical education is as important as intellectual education, and physical education is needed to maintain the *polis*'s security, both external and internal. Plato himself mentioned the kinds of physical education that should be experienced by young people, according to their current and future social status.

[6]Vassil Girginov and Jim Parry, *The Olympic Games Explained: A Student Guide to the Evolution of the Modern Olympic Games* (Oxford: Routledge, 2005), vi.

as the perception of the body included its function in the *polis*, the viability of which it was a crucial element. The body was perceived as a means through which political life was lived, or, as Foucault would have it, a means through the discipline of the political life was embodied in its agent, the 'man' or citizen, and which moulded his conscience.[7]

Consequently, during classical Greek antiquity, the body was perceived as a crucial element in the 'typical' procedures of the 'political' life, as having a clear political function and utility, since the body was simultaneously an agent of political power and subject to the discipline of the *polis* – the body was committed to the decisions of the *polis*.[8] So discipline was identified with body, since the body should be disciplined, enduring and committed, but only to what it had been decided to concede to the *polis*.

The medieval period and the sacred soul

In both the Eastern and Western medieval Christian traditions, the body was seen as the mortal vessel for the immortal soul. Because the body was tainted with 'original sin', physical exercise was not favoured in Christian education.[9] In the eastern-Byzantine-Orthodox tradition, which was cultivated in an *imperium* rather than a democracy, the body was not seen as a means to obtain pleasure, and bodily illness was a punishment from God for sins previously committed. Unlike in the ancient democratic tradition, the body was not seen as a vital part of the treasury of the *polis*, or as a guardian of it, and was no longer interwoven with political functions. As a result, in Byzantine education, centred on monasteries and the clergy, physical activities – and, in a broader sense, education for the body – were to be

---

[7]Michel Foucault, *Surveiller et punir. Naissance de la prison* (Athens: Kedros, Greek translation, 1979), 181–226; Graham Burchell, 'Peculiar Interests: Civic Society and Governing 'The System of Natural Liberty', in *The Foucault Effect: Studies in Governmentality*, ed. Graham Burchell, Collin Gordon and Peter Miller (Chicago: University of Chicago Press, 1991), 119–50, esp. 120–1; Michel Foucault, *Power/Knowledge: Selected Interviews and Other Writings, 1972–1977* (New York: Pantheon Books, 1980). The Foucauldian perspective, of course, focuses on the meaning of discipline exercised from the medieval period until the dawn of modernity (Foucault, *Power/Knowledge*, 39).

[8]Michel Foucault, *The Foucault Reader*, ed. Paul Rabinow (New York: Vintage Books, 2010); Mimi Orner, 'School Marks: Education, Domination and Female Subjectivity', in *Foucault's Challenge: Discourse, Knowledge and Power in Education*, ed. Thomas Popkewitz and Marie Brennan (New York: Teachers College, 1998), 278–94. Although Foucault himself strongly suggests the virility of Athenian *polis* as a core element (*The Foucault Reader*, 346–7), it should not be forgotten that the 'technology of the self' was another core element of political life in the Athenian *polis*, since 'the technologizing of the self happens in part through the stories we tell others and ourselves about who we are' (Orner, 280) and as Thucydides (2.37–41) proclaimed these stories were the base upon which the Athenian *polis* was constructed ('*who are we*' is question of much more importance than the 'we are *not* like them' aphorism). Nevertheless, it should be admitted that the whole story of the Olympics (and of other Games), and in a broader sense of the physical activities and the prominence of the body, is a gendered one, since women were abolished into the 'passive' regime (along with slaves) (*The Foucault Reader*, 345).

[9]Adrian Niculcea, 'Historical and Systematic Modern Observation concerning the "Filioque Addition"', *International Journal of Orthodox Theology* 1, no. 2 (2010): 96–116; Alexander Vasilev, *History of the Byzantine Empire*: Vol. 1, *324–1453* (Madison: University Of Wisconsin Press, 1952), 238.

avoided, if not wholly forbidden. Physical training was assigned only for soldiers, who guarded the borders of the empire.[10]

Later, during the Ottoman occupation of Greece (1453–1821), physical activities were exercised by paramilitary groups, which eventually fought in the Greek War of Independence (1821). It should be emphasised that these physical activities lacked the philosophical background of the ancient ones, and nor were they legitimised by the body's political functions: physical activities were led by the need for maintaining the physical power of the body in order to be ready for battle. The Byzantine-Orthodox educational tradition expressed its interest solely in the philosophical questions surrounding the 'soul', and matters of dogma.[11] In such a context education was detached from 'political' activities, and therefore the 'body' (as an entity and as a concept) was detached from the 'political' in favour of the salvation of the 'soul'.

The nineteenth and twentieth centuries: the political soul and the micro-physics of power

During the second half of the nineteenth century, when Greece was finally established as a free and independent State, education was formatted (1834–1847) by the Bavarian counsellors of King Otto, according to the Bavarian educational model.[12] However, physical education (PE) was introduced into the secondary education curriculum only in 1880, almost 50 years after the establishment of secondary education in 1836, and PE teachers' training was not initiated until 1882.[13] In the two years from 1880 to 1882 PE was taught in schools by fire brigade officers, who were the only people officially educated and trained in physical activities.[14] Despite

---

[10]Ioannis Markantonis, *Παραδόσεις στην ιστορία της Παιδείας* (*Lectures on the History of Paedia*) (Athens, 1981), 132.

[11]Jeremiah Heath Russell, 'Athens and Byzantium: Platonic Political Philosophy in Religious Empire' (unpublished PhD thesis, Louisiana State University, 2010).

[12]Government Gazette 87/31-12-1836; Sifis Bouzakis, *History of Modern Greek Education, 1821–1989* (Athens: Gutenberg, 1995), 40–44; Douglas Dakin, *The Unification of Greece 1770–1923*, Greek trans. A. Xanthopoulos (Athens: MIET, 1972), 108–16.

[13]Maria Karantaidou, *P.E. in Greek Secondary Education (1862–1990) and the Institutions for P.E. Teachers' Education (1882–1982)* (Thessaloniki: Kyriakidis Bros, 2000); Chronis Lamprou, 'P.E. Curricula of Primary and Secondary Education and Courses of Study for P. E. Teachers' Education in P.E. and Sports Faculties (1983–2008)' (unpublished PhD thesis, University of Athens/Greece, 2012), 73, 97. A fundamental distinction in terminology needs to be drawn here: due to the ideological perception of the direct succession of the modern Greek language from its ancient form, the terms 'gymnastics' and 'physical education' are traditionally used in Greek education as equal and identical, regardless of the differentiation of their meaning and content (especially in current literature of the field) (Karantaidou, 17). Since it is also mentioned that the 'theory of the ancient Greek model was identical to English sporting system' (Lamprou, 103), is not surprising the term 'sports' has been used in education simultaneously and alternatively to the terms PE and gymnastics. According to the 1975 Constitution Act and the 1976–1977 education reform law, the term 'PE' is preferred over the term 'gymnastics' to define the school subject, despite objections on the part of the Pedagogical Institute (the education authority). By the Act of 147/1976 (Government Gazette 56/1976) the (educational) PE Administration includes simultaneously PE projects and the school gymnastic activities. It is clear that the terminology around this school subject is highly disputable.

[14]Government Gazette 7/1871, Ministry of Education Directive 2147/8-4-1871 '*On Military Exercises for Pupils*' and Government Gazette 139/1883.

the establishment of a higher education academy for future secondary PE teachers, the course they studied lasted only 40 days.[15] After the first modern Olympic Games, in Athens in 1896, the education of PE teachers was extended to two years, so it could be argued that the rebirth of the Olympics was a landmark in the history of PE.[16] Law BXKA/1899 established the School of Gymnastic Teachers.

In 1907 Swedish gymnastics was adopted by school authorities as the most appropriate form of PE, and from 1918 the education for PE teachers was provided by the Gymnastic Academy. Later, in the educational reform of 1929, the Gymnastic Academy was recognised as a higher educational institution, equal in status with the Teachers' Academy (Law 4371/1929). The last reform of PE teachers' education was in 1982, when the Teachers' and Gymnastic Academies were incorporated into universities (Law 1268/1982), the period of study was increased to four years, and graduates' educational and social status – as 'PE teachers' – was restored.

Throughout the modern period, there has been a relationship between PE (and sport) and politics and ideology in Greek education. For example, in 1939, shortly before the Second World War, the Fascist government renamed the Gymnastic Academy the National Academy of Physical Education, with the emphasis on the 'National' (Law 2057/1939). Metaxas, the Fascist dictator, wanted to 'nationalise' the curriculum, in both PE and education more widely. After the war and the subsequent Greek civil war (1944–1949) there were other political and educational priorities, and PE remained largely as it had been in the 1930s. Only in the mid-1960s did a political-ideological turn result in a new focus on certain political aspects of PE.

During the dictatorship of the 'junta' (1967–1974), PE programmes were consistently referred to as 'gymnastics', in an attempt to legitimise the military regime through a direct reflection of the glories of Greek antiquity. During this period there were large and obligatory 'gymnastics exhibitions' in stadiums and squares, accompanied by military marches and festivities. Tanks and a heavily armed military presence in the streets were not unusual sights at this time. After the re-establishment of democracy in 1974–1975, the new government staged an 'educational reform', but this left PE untouched.[17]

A major change occurred as a result of the educational reform in 1982. The enhanced status of the Gymnastic Academy was followed by Law 1566/1982, which assigned the teaching of PE exclusively to graduates of the Academy, whose degrees were equivalent to others awarded in universities. This can be seen as a social recognition of the importance of the jobs done by PE teachers, but otherwise nothing else changed in Greek PE between 1950 and the mid-1980s.

In Greece today, PE programmes are implemented in schools as part of a broader national project, related to major events, particularly the 2004 Olympics or their aftermath: PE projects appear under the name *Kallipateira*, replacing the *Olympic Paideia* or *Olympische Bildung* project of 2004. None of these projects, however, has succeeded in diverting young people from unhealthy habits that result

---

[15]Law AXH/1887. See more details on this issue in Dakin, *The Unification of Greece*; Nicos Mouzelis, *Post-Marxist Alternatives*, Greek trans. Basil Kapetangiannis (Athens: Themelio, 1992).

[16]Karantaidou, *P.E. in Greek Secondary Education*, 31.

[17]Bouzakis, *History of Modern Greek Education*, 133–50.

in diabetes, obesity and related diseases. In Greece, 35% of the total population is obese, and 55% of school-age children (the third highest rate in the world), despite the huge efforts made both by the State and by PE teachers to promote such projects.[18]

As this brief historical survey has shown, in both ancient and modern Greece PE has borne the imprint of political ideology. A key question is whether PE is perceived as an autonomous school subject or must always be related to the major political and ideological agendas of the State. Political concerns have not disappeared from PE; they have only altered through time. As a result PE has been a means of discipline and of providing legitimacy to the political regime, whether this has been an extremist one such as the Fascist government of 1936–1941 or the junta of 1967–1974, or even the modern representative democracy. The next section will outline a theoretical and conceptual framework for analysing the development of the PE curriculum in its social context.

Theory and concepts

It is important to draw the distinction between PE as an autonomous subject and as the subject of a political and ideological agenda. Arguably, the PE curriculum ought to have as its direct and unquestionable objective the promotion of healthy habits and the enhancement of physical strength among pupils, with no intervention on behalf of 'political' or 'economic' agendas. In this conception, the content of the PE curriculum has no direct correspondence with the legitimising functions of other subjects taught in schools. The PE curriculum, however, corresponds to an ideological agenda: as Foucault showed, the functions of the body can be adapted into a political doctrine or ideology and be manipulated according to it, and the body can be subjected to a variety of controls.[19] This relationship between the body and power must be investigated thoroughly from a multidisciplinary perspective. As Foucault explained, power 'reaches into the very grain of individuals, touches their bodies and inserts itself into their actions and attitudes, their discourses, learning processes and everyday lives', while the 'regime of power' exercises it within the social body.[20]

If, as Foucault observes, 'the body is the inscribed surface of events',[21] it is important to attempt to understand the ways in which power is inscribed into citizens and how power succeeds in mobilising – or immobilising – them. The key question, at a theoretical level, is who controls and is benefited by such an operation of power.[22] In the classical Marxist approach, the 'superstructure' is a reflection of, and is determined by, the 'base': the latter is the economic structure, while the

---

[18]For further details on this issue see Efthimios Kapantais et al., 'First National Epidemiological Large-scale Survey on the Prevalence of Obesity in Greek Adults', *International Journal of Obesity* 28 (2004): 72; George Koukoulis et al., 'High Rates of Obesity Prevalence in Adults living in Central Greece: Data from the ARGOS Study', *Hormones* 9, no. 3 (2010): 253–62; Ioannis Kyriazis et al., 'Obesity Indicators in Pupils of Elementary Education in Urban Areas of Attiki Prefecture', *Archives of Hellenic Medicine* 27, no. 6 (2010): 937–43.

[19]Foucault, *Power/Knowledge*, 100–2.

[20]Foucault, *Power/Knowledge*, 39.

[21]Foucault, *The Foucault Reader*, 83.

[22]Foucault, *Power/Knowledge*, 102.

former is considered to be everything else, including the political system, the system of ideas, schools, the police, religion, the armed forces, and so on.[23] The superstructure develops in such a way as to legitimise the base – to manipulate and even 'discipline' those who might question the status of the social establishment. According to Althusser's notorious distinction, there are two kinds of mechanism that the superstructure has developed to do this: the disciplinary and the ideological, which are both established to ensure the maintenance of the 'base' and to guarantee its reproduction. This is, ultimately, the function of the superstructure.[24]

Schools and the schooling system have a distinguished place among the ideological mechanisms of social reproduction; their primary aim is to provide a solid legitimisation and a deep 'understanding' of the social establishment, in other words to incorporate 'individuals' into society as 'members' who will accept social hierarchies, inequalities and distortions as they are.[25] To do so, education – structured, controlled and manipulated by the bourgeoisie, as the theory explains – focuses on particular areas of knowledge, and this 'school-knowledge', incorporated into bourgeois ideology and ways of life, is infiltrated into curricula and thus disseminated throughout society.[26] Curricula, therefore, are considered part of the bourgeois agenda for political and ideological domination. It seems, from the structuralist point of view, that the core elements of the dominant ideology are incorporated into school-knowledge, which penetrates society via all social institutions, thereby legitimising the social order.[27]

However, according to Mouzelis's analysis of post-Marxist perspectives, it should be theoretically possible for the field of political production to be in a state of absolute autonomy. The political field – and its needs for production and reproduction – may predominate, especially in certain cases where state formation did not follow the 'typical' Western path, whereby the economy and its needs for production and reproduction were the dominant social facts and the whole social structure was based upon them. In cases like these, especially in 'peripheral' states

---

[23]The basic scheme was proposed by Marx and was excessively illustrated by Althusser's structuralist perspective. See Luis Althusser, 'Idéologie et appareils idéologiques d'État (notes pour une recherche)', *La Pensée* 151 (1970): 3–38. For a critique on this methodological thesis see briefly: Foucault, *Power/Knowledge*, 78–108; Mouzelis, *Post-Marxist Alternatives*.

[24]Althusser, *Idéologie et appareils idéologiques d'État*.

[25]Althusser, '*Idéologie et appareils idéologiques d'État*'; Michael Apple, *Cultural and Economic Reproduction in Education: Essays on Class, Ideology and the State* (London: Routledge & Kegan Paul, 1982); Basil Bernstein, 'Class and Pedagogies: Visible and Invisible', in *Power and Ideology in Education*, ed. Jerome Karabel and Albert Henry Halsey (New York: Oxford University Press, 1977), 511–34; Basil Bernstein, *Pedagogy, Symbolic Control and Identity: Theory, Research, Critique* (London: Taylor & Francis, 1996); Samuel Bowles, 'Unequal Education and Reproduction of the Social Division of Labor', in *Power and Ideology in Education*, ed. Jerome Karabel and Albert Henry Halsey (New York: Oxford University Press, 1977), 137–53.

[26]Basil Bernstein, *Pedagogic codes and Social Control*, ed. and trans. Joseph Solomon (Athens: Alexandria 1992); Bernstein, *Pedagogy, Symbolic Control and Identity*.

[27]Althusser, 'Idéologie et appareils idéologiques d'État'; Apple, *Cultural and Economic Reproduction in Education*; Bernstein, *Pedagogy, Symbolic Control and Identity*.

such as the Balkans or Latin America, where the political field and its needs prevailed over any others, and the dominant agents of the political fields prevailed over the needs of any others and were the socially dominant agents, it was possible for the political dimension to prevail over even the economic.[28] Here, ideology is used to legitimise the political mode of production instead of legitimising, as in the classical Marxist understanding, the economic mode of production.

In a case such as that of the Greek State, established in the early nineteenth century with specific features – both social and economic – that do not match the model of Western state formation, it is not clear whether the formal structuralist approach is the appropriate one, or whether another explanatory model should be adopted.

Analysis and outcomes

This article examines PE curricula in Greek secondary education. They are analysed using Bernstein's conceptual tools of 'framing' and 'classification', which allow us to deconstruct them and reveal the implicit underlying conditions of their construction, ideologies and connection to political agendas.[29] 'Framing' consists of the pedagogy assigned to certain activities, mostly the boundaries between 'what can' and 'what cannot' be presented in any form of educational activity. 'Classification' consists of boundaries between subjects, both in science and at the school level, and the hierarchy assigned to those subjects in particular places and at particular times. Deconstructing and decoding curricula using this conceptual framework can reveal the nature of knowledge conducted into society, and can provide insights into who really controlled this process. In this case, it helps us to ask whether PE is implemented in schools solely for strengthening the body and developing healthy habits, or for reasons related to political and ideological indoctrination; moreover, it can explain whether this political and ideological indoctrination, if it occurs, is driven by the bourgeois will to expand its domination, or by other motors. Simultaneously, content analysis provides us with key insights into the aims and content of the curricula, by allowing us to scrutinise the 'discourse' underlying curriculum construction. Categorising certain keywords as 'educational' or 'political', and measuring their use, will reveal the nature of the content of curricula. Words that might not be reasonably expected to be present, or dominant, in a school PE curriculum – such as 'nation', 'ethics', 'tradition' and its synonyms, 'ancient' and so on – are seen as indicators of a political and ideological agenda. Others are counted as having an educational meaning and purpose.

The objectives – the philosophical and didactic perspectives – of PE curricula are also analysed, considering the methodological directions given to those teaching

---

[28]Nicos Mouzelis, *Parliamentarism and Industrialization in Semi-peripheral States: Greece, Balkans, Latin America*, Greek trans. Basil Kapetangiannis (Athens: Themelio, 1987).
[29]These tools and their utilities are analysed extensively in Bernstein, *Pedagogic Codes and Social Control*; Bernstein, *Pedagogy, Symbolic Control and Identity*.

the syllabus. These objectives are usually abstract,[30] but can be revealed through the directives addressed to teachers.[31] Content analysis will reveal whether or not the curricular philosophical objectives were aligned with teaching directives.

Greek PE curricula

'Classification' and 'framing' from the 1950s to the 2000s

Using the concepts of framing and classification, it can be seen that the subject of PE in schools was given a low priority, ranked at the bottom of the list of school subjects and given a low number of teaching hours, for almost the whole period in question. In the 1950s and 1960s it was in the lowest position of all subjects in the school curriculum, except during the dictatorship of the junta, when it was third from the bottom. PE fitted into the 'arts and senses' group of school subjects,[32] which has usually been at the bottom of the hierarchy, perceived by both teachers and students as 'peripheral' rather than 'hard-core'. The discrimination between these two types of subject has resulted in a severe distortion throughout elementary and high-school education, with the lower-ranked subjects – and those assigned to teach them – labelled as 'peripheral' and 'marginal'. This in turn has resulted in a disdainful attitude to these subjects on the part of pupils, a low level of confidence among the teachers, and ultimately the nullifying of their curricular objectives.

PE was, and is, among these subjects, and PE teachers know that their subject is poorly evaluated by pupils, often seen as a quasi-voluntary 'play-zone'. Teachers' requests for a 'sports dress code' have rarely been accepted – too often pupils 'forget' to bring their sports kit to school. There is strong pressure on teachers to give their pupils high grades, particularly in high schools, because high grades are the benchmark for admission to university.[33] PE teachers are rarely involved in school interdisciplinary activities, and PE is not attractive to other school teachers who are devising interdisciplinary projects. This situation supports Bernstein's concept of 'classification': strong disciplinary borders have been established, and PE is perceived as a 'unique' – non-theoretical and non-academic, and therefore

---

[30]Ioannis Vrettos, 'The Reliability and Legitimacy Problem in Decision Making during the Curriculum Formation', *Pedagogic Review* 3 (1985): 115–34, esp. 117, 120; Panagiotis Xochelis, 'The Curriculum Modernization Problem', *Philologist* 23 (1981): 265–71; Nicos Terzis, 'Viewpoints on Educational Reform', *Philologist* 23 (1981): 272–81; Ioannis Vrettos and Andreas Kapsalis, *Curriculum: Theory and Know-how for Planning and Reforming* (Athens: Ellinika Grammata, 1990), 97, 168. Dimitrios Charalampus, 'Educational Policy and Educational Reform in Post-war Greece (1950–1974)' (unpublished PhD thesis, University of Thessaloniki/Greece, 1990), 119.

[31]George Flouris, 'Disharmony between Educational Legislation, Curriculum, School Textbooks and Teaching: An Aspect of Greek Educational Crisis', in *World Crisis in Education*, ed. Ioannis Pyrgiotakis and Ioannis Kanakis (Athens: Gregory, 1999), 206–39.

[32]Charalampos Noutsos, *Curricula and Social Control* (Athens: Themelio, 1988); Panagiotis Persians, *School Knowledge in Secondary Education, 1823–1929* (Athens: Gregory, 2000); Dimitris Foteinos, *History and Comparative History of the Greek Secondary Curricula, 1950–1977* (published PhD thesis, University of Patras/Greece, 2004);George Flouris, *Curricula for a New Era in Education* (Athens: Gregory, 2005).

[33]The Greek education system is highly exercise-oriented. The common excuse pupils address to PE teachers goes more or less like this: 'Come on, do you think it's fair to get a low grade from you and not gain admission to university just because I'm lazy in sports?'. An overwhelming moral dilemma for PE teachers.

peripheral – subject. It is not surprising that the scheduled teaching time for PE is among the lowest, compared with other school subjects: only music and 'arts' get a little less.

More serious limitations arose from the legislative status of PE. The law imposed on teachers a certain schedule and certain requirements of behaviour concerning their relations with their pupils. It did not take account of the differences in facilities between schools, differences between teachers, or the diversity of pupils' abilities. Teachers were seen as having a specific role, in both school and society, determined by the script of a curriculum that neither they nor their pupils had any authority to alter. A uniformity of activities was suggested by the PE curriculum, which had to be implemented. Moreover, the major PE programme, at least until the end of the 1980s, was based on Swedish gymnastics; it was a rather static programme, and one could easily come to the conclusion that PE was not a favoured subject among pupils, who probably wanted to be more active and self-acting than a 'simple' Swedish gymnastic programme would permit.

'Classification' and 'framing' from c.2000 to 2008

The Swedish gymnastic programme lasted until the mid-1980s. Thereafter a new version of the PE programme was initiated through the curricular reform which occurred at this time, recognising the pupils' needs for physical exercise, and for mental and emotional development along with the social need for healthiness, an expressed need of Greek society in the new millennium. The new PE curriculum admitted the complexity of its didactic objectives, and therefore presented these as expanding in three dimensions: cognition, skills and attitudes. For the PE curriculum these were 'translated' as:

- 'cognition': a quasi-encyclopaedic learning of the history of several sports, or learning their present rules and cultures; understanding the social and individual effects that sports can have; promotion of healthy habits and hobbies;
- 'psycho-kinetics': for example, the cultivation of rhythm, strength, power and speed, and development of the ability for multi-complex moves;
- 'attitude': developing social goals, such as the abilities of teamwork, tolerance, self-confidence, patience, courage, and self-control, and moral ones such as honesty, justice, fair play, respect for the opposition, moderation in victory and defeat, and so on.

Entering the new millennium, the Greek capital Athens was nominated as the host of 2004 Olympic Games, and the already renewed PE curriculum had once more to be updated under the new perspectives. A new PE and sports programme named *Olympic Paedeia* (*Olympische Bildung*) was launched, adding a few new characteristics (such as sports courses) to the PE curriculum in use. In reality, this was just the reinvention of existing sports (those in the Olympic Games) and of the PE curriculum, with an emphasis on the virtues of fair play, tolerance and compassion, and on the holistic approach of the ancient Greeks, who combined physical and intellectual achievements.

Despite the new didactic approach adopted by curriculum developers, the *Olympic Paedeia* programme did not change much in respect of 'classification' and 'framing'. PE remained in the lowest ranked place among school subjects in elementary education, and as for the relations between different subjects, the boundaries have remained as hard as they were previously. According to the *Olympia Paedeia* programme, PE should have developed through interdisciplinary projects, but the directions for the implementation of the programme set aside only one teaching hour for PE, and this during the 'flexible zone' of the curriculum.[34] It is not an uncommon situation: curricular objectives, philosophically determined and arbitrarily manifested, were undermined by the direct instructions given to teachers.[35] These excessively detailed instructions turned the curriculum into a strict legislative enactment that left no room for innovation or initiatives, despite the objectives of the curriculum that claimed the exact opposite.

Surprisingly, the secondary education curriculum, particularly that of the senior high schools, places PE in the highest rank that it has ever had. In the second grade of senior high school, PE is ranked in third place and has 2/32 of the total teaching hours per week, following the subjects of religion and a foreign language. However, in the third grade PE is downgraded to the fourth rank, with 1/31 of the total teaching hours, and falls behind Ancient Greek language and literature.

This improved position in the hierarchy of subjects raises the question of whether, under the *Olympic Paedeia*, PE had at last found a respected place in the curriculum, or whether this improvement was coincidental. This can be partly answered using the 'framing' concept. Although the new programme expected innovation and initiatives on the part of PE teachers, this was not presented as different from earlier curricula. Meanwhile, there were excessively detailed directions for teachers, even to the level of descriptions of the exact way in which exercises should be correctly executed, and there was also a very detailed teaching plan to be followed by all teachers.[36] For students, this resulted in a real distortion of the meaning of PE: they had a book! Under the *Olympic Paedeia* programme, pupils had a PE textbook, which can be seen as indoctrinating rather than informative. They had to learn almost everything about the Olympics: the textbook reveals an evident urge to 'mould' an 'Olympic conscience'. Pupils were required to internalise the ideology of the Olympics, to behave 'properly' and to adapt to the environment that the Games were intended to enhance. Much of the PE textbook focused on notions and ideals, manners and attitudes.[37]

Given the low amount of teaching time assigned to PE, especially for the third grade of the senior high schools – one teaching period to cover sports and kinetics, physical exercise and the *Olympic Paedeia* elements of the curriculum – it seems clear that the boundaries of 'framing' were very tight.

The programme that was initiated after the Games, from 2004 to 2008, was called *Kallipateira*. This was really just a change of name, and continued the indoctrination of the ideas developed during *Olympic Paedeia*. The objectives of

---

[34]Andreas Tassinos, 'Our Educational System is Unprepared to Accept the "Flexible Zone"', *Scientific Tribune* 10 (2009). The 'flexible zone' is a time-zone of a quasi-school/class-based curriculum, which, however, was used – in the 'real' world of the school daily routine – for maths and language tutoring. These extra hours, offered by the State to schools, for innovation and interdisciplinary projects, were, finally, used for *simple tutoring*, abolishing any didactic and pedagogic benefits that could ensue from it).

[35]Flouris, 'Disharmony'.

[36]*Olympic Paideia: From Theory to Practice* (Athens: Ministry of Education and the Organizing committee of the 'Athens 2004' Olympic Games, 2001), 114.

[37]Ibid., 113, 120–1.

Kallipateira concerned the promotion of equality among people of all races, colours, religions and sexual orientations, the enhancement of tolerance towards 'difference', and adaptation to an 'open, tolerant and democratic society of a globalised and multicultural world'.[38] It is not actually clear whether *Kallipateira* is still in progress or whether it has been cancelled: there was no formal announcement that it had ended, though it was explicitly designed to be active until 2008. What remains for the time being is a PE programme, whatever its name might be, taught 'by the book', aimed more at indoctrination than sporting achievement, taught in a limited amount of time (especially in senior high schools), under excessively detailed curricular instructions addressed to both teachers and pupils, and operated recently within very strict funding limitations.

Content analysis

The PE curricula from the 1950s to the 1970s were a blend of abstraction in general aims and detail in specific instructions to teachers.[39] One document announced that 'physical education is aiming to enhance the psychophysical development of pupils, to enhance their physical abilities and promote their mental health'. These targets would be implemented by 'a maximum 10 minutes game of throwing and catching the ball', or by swimming activities,[40] or by dancing exercises (aiming to familiarise pupils with the steps of traditional Greek dances).[41] There were also directions for 'running up to 100 metres' in groups, and even strict instructions on how to play the game 'who is afraid of the Negro'.[42] The innovative part of this curriculum asked teachers to invent some exercises and relate them to national myths or events. The instructions addressed to PE teachers were very strict and detailed concerning the physical motions that pupils should perform – exactly how to move the leg, arm, and so on; how many centimetres the limb concerned should be moved; how the body should be positioned. It appears that the State in this period, as reflected in the curriculum, did not appreciate the professional status of PE teachers, and thought them in need of instruction in the basics of their jobs. The most amusing part of the curriculum advised PE teachers to keep pupils indoors during rainy days and teach them about road safety measures.

The PE curriculum of the dictatorship (1967–1974) also focused on the cultivation of love for nature (the nature of the 'fatherland'), and of moral virtues and ethical behaviour. It also explicitly suggested that one of the main objectives of PE was

---

[38]*Press Bulletin of 7-02-2006* (Athens: Ministry of Education).

[39]See also Flouris, 'Disharmony'.

[40]This is projected as an optional didactic tool, when no public school has – even today– a swimming pool, and even some of the middle-class/rank private schools do not have one either.

[41]Teaching of dances has an ideological perspective: it would be inappropriate for a Greek student not to be able to dance when it was needed. And this was basically the case for school exhibitions, during the closing-for-summer school ceremony, when students ought to perform dances, honouring the ancestors and their glorious past, the traditions that moulded the newly formed State's identity. The legislative purpose is also served: the newly formed State is the unquestionable continuation of the ancient (and medieval) State. Therefore, the spirit of the past is vivid in the nation's present. But if this is not an ideological usage of the PE curriculum, what else would be?

[42]Government Gazette 347-1977.

to maintain tradition and the holistically perceived 'national spirit'.[43] The objectives went beyond those that common sense would expect from PE. During the dictatorship, there were also military-style exercises, with marches and marching formations, the aim being to keep 'pupils in continuous motion and activities' during the teaching hour in order to 'keep them constantly busy'. Physical activities were used to prepare pupils for a potential future national emergency, all excessively detailed and explicitly declared in the curriculum objectives. Content analysis of the 1967–1974 PE curriculum reveals the power of 'framing': there are 11 pages of excessively detailed orders and directions for PE activities in the curriculum, strengthening the control by the State over both teachers and pupils.

The structure of the PE curriculum lasted until the arrival of the Olympic Games in Athens, which the State decided would be an opportunity to renew the old-fashioned curriculum. In addition, with the eyes of the international community on Greece, it was felt that some of the Greek people should know something more about the sports that were hitherto not well known in Greece, such as baseball and badminton. To enhance the 'spirit of the Games', the *Olympic Paedeia* curriculum was devised, partly changing the perception of PE. Swedish gymnastics were abandoned, and new sports were included, and the political and ideological framework also changed. Instead of cultivating 'love for the fatherland' through the PE curriculum, tolerance towards the *allotrio* was encouraged – the person from another place who is not a familiar figure. Another aim was tolerance towards the 'ones with less', as the motto of the new curriculum – as presented on the cover page of the textbook – was 'all different, all equal – from sports to everyday life'. This was a new perception, a new translation of the 'Olympic spirit', adapted to the needs of the modern globalised world, the world of multicultural societies, non-governmental organisations and voluntary community work.[44]

These may be laudable aspirations, promoting a virtuous moral agenda, but the key question is: what do they have to do with PE? In addition, would a PE curriculum based on these ideas have a higher rank among the school subjects?

To look at this new (2004–2008) curriculum in terms of 'classification', it can be noted that the position of PE did not alter, either for better or for worse, in either elementary or junior secondary education – it remained the lowest-ranked of all subjects. At senior secondary level, the spatial boundaries of 'classification' were loosened, up to a point, and the PE curriculum incorporated hygiene. Chapters on healthy sexual behaviour were included in the textbook, with information on venereal diseases and material on discrimination based on sexual orientation. The basics of 'leisure management' were also taught. However, the well-known and familiar aspects of PE also appeared: national dances, the traditions of the 'fatherland' and so on.

In this curriculum, PE was the third-ranked subject; this can be explained by the curriculum content of 'sports and physical education'. These programmes, *Olympic Paedeia* and *Kallipateira*, were taught in a less physical and practical way, and more academically, and thus the proper place of PE was among the school subjects with an ideological content. Yet at the same time there was a severe reduction of the scheduled teaching hours available for PE. The content, then, was upgraded while the subject per se was downgraded. This seems to show that the subject's

---

[43]Government Gazette 218-1969.
[44]*Olympic Paedia*, 13–23.

content was seen to have a crucial ideological dimension, but this dimension could be better served through other – more 'important' and less 'peripheral' – school subjects.

In terms of 'framing', it is important to be aware of a broad movement for educational reform during the past five years. New laws, new ideas and a desire to follow fashionable global trends have all characterised this movement. There has been a strengthening of central control over education, and a weakening of teachers' autonomy; the individual has become increasingly immobilised. The question remains, however, as to whether these reforms are expressing the real needs of the bourgeois class in Greece, or whether they must be considered as parts of mechanisms servicing the goals of other agents of social action.

Some conclusions

As has been evident throughout this brief outline of Greek PE curriculum history, the 'political' has always been a key aspect of school knowledge construction. It also seems to be evident that educational policy-makers, instead of developing a 'sound body' – with a knowledge of its functions, restrictions and possibilities, oriented towards healthy habits – were constantly having as an objective of PE the cultivation of a sound 'political soul', involving the indoctrination into pupils of national ideals, which in turn helped to form personal identities. By moulding each personal identity with the doctrines of political legitimisation, the person becomes manipulated, disciplined and controllable.

The key question posed in this article was whether PE is perceived as an autonomous school subject, aimed at strengthening the body and promoting a healthy life, or whether it must be related to the major political and ideological agendas of the state. In light of the circumstances mentioned above, it should be noted that the 'image' of the body, from the perception of PE in antiquity to the present, has undoubtedly changed, because the content of the 'political' has changed. In Ancient Greece the body was 'organically' integrated into the functions of the *polis* and its political procedures, and therefore the body was political.[45] The body had/was a political entity, an entity that was active in order to be capable of managing every aspect of public life, and it was mobilised towards these. Even when delegating to the *polis* certain of its individual rights – and becoming itself dispensable – the body was still political, because it was oriented towards the functions and needs of the *polis*. The knowledge produced from the political body returned to the *polis*, strengthening its regime of power. In the Byzantine period the body per se was separated from the soul, as public life was dissociated from private life; the public and the *polis* were detached from the administration of public life. Consequently, as the body was not a necessary element for managing public life, only the soul needed to be moulded, as a political soul; as Foucault claimed, the soul, the disciplined self, the prison of the body, is the core on which discipline is inscribed, through the rules and norms of the judicial system.[46]

Since the body in the public sphere has been immobilised, detached from its essence and from the ability to control the knowledge and the power it was produc-

---

[45]See Emile Durkheim, *Division of Labor in Society* , trans. L. Coser (New York: Free Press, 1984). As Durkheim noted, it is a clear example of 'mechanical solidarity'.
[46]Foucault, *Surveiller et punir*.

ing by itself, it was inevitable that the body in education, and consequently in PE, would be immobilised. It is not surprising, therefore, that a textbook was introduced for PE under the *Olympic Paedeia* curriculum, with students having to be seated during the PE class! In present times, the body is excluded from most political functions, as representative or parliamentary democracy is the new dominant political tradition (size of population is always a good excuse for exclusion from direct political participation). However, this exclusion left enough space for indoctrination and disciplining ideologies to penetrate the social body, creating a 'political soul' – but soul, as Foucault claimed, is the indoctrinated and disciplined self.

Therefore, the relation between PE and the 'political' was not diminished at all, but only altered. Discipline was produced by the 'micro-physics of power';[47] the body as an agent of power was marginalised, as it had lost its relation to the political and remained only as a disciplined figure conceding almost all of its rights to its representatives. When representative democracy was under siege by the Fascist regime or the military junta these rights perished completely. It was inevitable, under this perspective, that the perception of the body and its political functions would be transformed, and the interweaving relationship between PE and political ideology would be altered.

It seems clear that school subjects, even those less obviously related to the dominant political ideology, acquire strict indoctrinating content and are attached to the political agenda of their time – and this has been true of PE. This is evident in both the authoritarian regimes and in the period of representative democracy. Both the authoritarian regimes – apart from what they did to society overall with the complete denial of political and individual rights, and the abolition of political freedom, and apart from their general educational legislation – had a particular relationship to 'gymnastics', as they called PE, and treated it more as an ideological tool than as a means to promote bodily strength and healthy habits. PE was a means to 'produce' ideology and legitimisation through its relation to antiquity. The regimes were legitimised by a direct connection between their own ideological and political agenda and their specifically moulded perception of antiquity. PE was one of the means by which this connection was made, and there was not an urge for objectives other than those of indoctrination. The enhancement of physical strength and promotion of healthy habits were less important to these regimes.

During the Third Democracy – since 1974 – a similar set of interwoven relationships between politics, their legitimisation and school subjects (in our case PE) is apparent. The major event that could draw attention to PE was, undoubtedly, the Olympic Games of 2004. Under the pressure of this global event, new educational material was introduced into schools, despite the tremendous amount of human and financial resources required. The *Olympic Paedeia* project, developed in the context of an updated pedagogic and didactic environment, nevertheless did not align itself with new educational concepts, and there was a divergence between its philosophical objectives and their actual implementation in the PE curriculum. The existence of such a divergence was the outcome of the relationship between visions of antiquity and the needs of contemporary globalised work: Greek policy-makers claimed

---

[47]Bob Jessop, 'From Micro-powers to Governmentality: Foucault's Work on Statehood, State Formation, Statecraft and State Power', *Political Geography* 26 (2007): 34–40.

that the new millennium would see the reincarnation of the glorious past in the modern world.[48] To do this, the perception of PE needed to be altered: new concepts, new ideas and new content had to be taught, and there would be no deviations from the politically assigned objectives. Therefore, in the case of the PE curriculum, the moulding of the political soul has prevailed over the strengthening of the Greek body: the body becomes dispensable again, but without a prior delegation on behalf of the 'actor'.

Within the school curriculum, in terms of both 'classification' and 'framing', boundaries are strengthened when there is a strong political agenda to be implemented, as in the case of the 2004–2008 curriculum, or when this agenda is functioning as a technology for political domination, as in the case of the two authoritarian regimes. In the latter cases, one can see that the PE curriculum was strengthening the boundaries of classification and framing, having as an objective to diminish, if not to eliminate, the possibility of intervention by non-politically-dominant agents. The reinvention of PE as a suitable technology during the 2004 agenda seems to be evidence of the ways in which politics can be exercised, through PE as a school subject, fortifying the legitimacy offered to the regime.

One could reasonably argue, therefore, that due to historical circumstances it could be inevitable that education in Greece would be highly oriented towards ideology, but the nature of this orientation needs to be closely examined. As far as PE is concerned, the ideological orientation of the curriculum seems inefficient and inappropriate to accomplish the objectives of PE, even those that are attributed, in abstract form, in the curriculum. As Foucault emphasised,[49] it is important to ask who controls and benefits from the curriculum, even the PE curriculum. It is not clear whether the structuralist explanation of historical change is the most suitable for cases such as Greece, where school curricula have been highly subject to ideological influence. This question should be asked, however, and requires further investigation using a wider range of sources.

---

[48]*Olympic Paedia*, 13; Flouris, 'Disharmony'.

[49]Foucault, *Power/Knowledge*, 102.

Index

Note: Page numbers in *italic* type refer to figures and illustrations